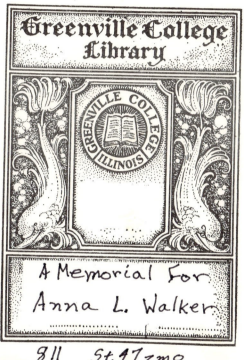

Wallace Stevens

IMAGINATION
AND FAITH

Princeton Essays in Literature

Advisory Committee: Joseph Bauke, Robert Fagles,
Claudio Guillén, Robert Maguire

For a listing of titles, see page 205

Wallace Stevens

IMAGINATION
AND FAITH

ADALAIDE KIRBY MORRIS

Princeton University Press
Princeton, New Jersey

Copyright © 1974 by Princeton University Press
Published by Princeton University Press, Princeton and London

All Rights Reserved.

Publication of this book has been aided by
a grant from the A. W. Mellon Foundation.

Library of Congress Cataloging in Publication Data will
be found on the last printed page of this book.

This book has been composed in Linotype Janson.

Printed in the United States of America
by Princeton University Press,
Princeton, New Jersey

Second Printing, 1975

for DAVID

CONTENTS

Acknowledgments

Poetry, as Stevens remarks, is not personal; nor can criticism be a private feat. I am thankful for the thoughtful advice and encouragement of Professors Samuel H. Monk and George T. Wright, for a generous loan of books from Professor Edward L. Kessler, and to Jenny Frazer for her deft and loyal assistance in preparing the manuscript for publication. Grateful acknowledgment is extended to Alfred A. Knopf, Inc. for the use of copyrighted material from the works of Wallace Stevens.

I would especially like to acknowledge the thorough, unwavering, and saving support of my husband, who made this, as only he could, a book scrivened in delight, for David.

ABBREVIATIONS

For brevity and convenience, references to Stevens'
poetry and prose are documented in parentheses within
the text. The following abbreviations, now traditional
in Stevens criticism, are used:

CP — *The Collected Poems of Wallace Stevens.*
New York: Alfred A. Knopf, 1954.

OP — *Opus Posthumous.* Ed., with an Introduction,
by Samuel French Morse. New York:
Alfred A. Knopf, 1957.

NA — *The Necessary Angel: Essays on Reality and
the Imagination.* New York: Alfred A. Knopf,
1951.

LWS — *Letters of Wallace Stevens.* Selected and
Edited by Holly Stevens. New York:
Alfred A. Knopf, 1966.

Wallace Stevens

IMAGINATION
AND FAITH

What makes the poet the potent figure that he is, or was,
or ought to be, is that he creates the world to which
we turn incessantly and without knowing it and
that he gives to life the supreme fictions without which
we are unable to conceive of it.

(NA 31)

INTRODUCTION

Shall our blood fail? Or shall it come to be
The blood of paradise? And shall the earth
Seem all of paradise that we shall know?

(CP 68)

STEVENS' rhetorical question in "Sunday Morning" con-
ceals the imperative of a skeptic and a naturalist: the earth
must be all of paradise, for it is all we have. At the same
time the question implies, through the word "fail," a
morality: we, who are all poets, that is to say men of
imagination, *can* make our blood the blood of paradise.

Sidestepping "a monumental explanation of [his] religion," Stevens described himself to Bernard Heringman
as "a dried-up Presbyterian" (LWS 792). He believed, to
the point of repetition, that "the death of one god," for
instance Phoebus, "is the death of all" (CP 381/OP 165),
for instance God the Father, the Son, and the Holy Ghost.
Stevens elevated poetry to take the place of "empty
heaven and its hymns" (CP 167). In a skeptical age, he
argued, "the mind turns to its own creations and examines
them, not alone from the aesthetic point of view, but for
what they reveal, for what they validate and invalidate"
(OP 159). Again and again he described poetry as a "sanction" for life:[1] poetry decrees our cosmic isolation, at
once a curse and a nobility; it impels moral action and
determines moral judgment; and, in a third meaning of

---

[1] See, for instance, NA 35, 43, and 173, LWS 299 and 600, and CP
239-240.

"sanction," it is a means of influencing society. The poet is the realist with a spiritual role, the man who "gives to life the supreme fictions without which we are unable to conceive of it" (NA 31).

Stevens once claimed that "the imagination is the next greatest power to faith" (NA 171), but in his writing he is always on the verge of a more blasphemous claim, one making faith the next greatest power to imagination. Imagination is the source of all religion, the origin of all belief. The poet is the spokesman for imagination, and, therefore, "it is he that invented the Gods. It is he that put into their mouths the only words they have ever spoken" (OP 167). This new formulation has two implications. The first is that, as Stevens noted in the "Adagia," "it is the belief and not the god that counts" (OP 162); therefore, it is only necessary to find a sufficient fiction, one which we may recognize as a fiction and yet feel to be an exquisite truth. If this is so, then the second implication is that aesthetics can no longer be independent of faith. It can, in fact, become "immeasurably a greater thing than religion" (OP 166).

J. V. Cunningham maintains that certain of Stevens' poems convey "a religious experience without the content of traditional religion,"[2] yet, this study will argue, as the Supreme Fiction overthrew the Supreme Being, it assumed many of the accoutrements of traditional religion. By endowing the physical with spiritual significance, the church, for Stevens' ancestors the Zellers and for Stevens himself in his youth, made the visible and the invisible one. In his more skeptical maturity, Stevens did not hesitate to search its forms for those of his poetic

[2] *Tradition and Poetic Structure* (Denver: Alan Swallow, 1960), p. 115.

religion, a fiction which, like all things new, thrust two ways: toward an implicit critique of the old (that which is corrected) and toward an explicit formulation of the new (that which is constructed).

The old is Stevens' heritage. In contrast to So-and-So reclining on her couch, Stevens was not born "at twenty-one, / Without lineage or language" (CP 295). The first chapter of this study, "Lineage and Language: Stevens' Religious Heritage," considers the forces of Stevens' background which made him turn instinctively to religion for sanction and solace. Whereas So-and-So's couch is ornamental, two-dimensional, part of a pose, the bed of old John Zeller, Stevens' inheritance, is fundamental, fully formed, part of a tradition. Zeller's faith, its forms and symbols, helped to determine Stevens' modes and methods of thought.

Stevens, however, was skeptical of these modes. The second chapter, "The Deaf-Mute Church and the Chapel of Breath," concerns Stevens' critique of the old faith and his efforts to construct a new, personal, and more expansive one, and the third chapter, "A Mystical Theology: Stevens' Poetic Trinity," considers the core of this new faith. Stevens' poetic trinity is a transvaluation of the Christian trinity. In his poetic doctrine, God becomes one with the imagination; Christ becomes the poet-hero, or incarnation of imagination; and the Holy Ghost becomes the active though diffused presence of imagination in human life.

"If poetry should address itself to the same needs and aspirations, the same hopes and fears, to which the Bible addresses itself," Stevens reasoned, "it might rival it in distribution" (NA 144). "Distribution" here seems to mean relevance as well as widespread dispersal, and, although Stevens quickly and rather unconvincingly hedges his statement with the certainty that "the Biblical imagination is one thing and the poetic imagination, inevitably, something else" (NA 144), he strives in his poetry to make the Supreme Fiction as immediately relevant to us as the Bible to the Zellers. The fourth chapter, "How to Live, What to Do," considers Stevens' reformulations of the religious history, personae, rites, and cosmology now stiffened into dogma. If God is the imagination, then biblical history becomes personal history: Genesis the moment of awareness which creates the world through the word of the poem; the Fall the moment of self-awareness which separates us from the world; grace, as in "The Sense of the Sleight-of-Hand Man," the moment of fortuitous delight suddenly available through an unmerited, natural (not divine) assistance. In the same way, biblical personae become aspects of our being. "The sum of our faculties," Stevens' "best definition" (NA 61) for imagination, includes all personae in potentiality. When, therefore, man's reason intrudes on reality, he is Adam; projecting his ego onto reality, he is Eve; denying the divinity of the world, he is Satan. Man, Stevens affirms, "can / Do all that angels can" (CP 405).

Yet he must do more. Unlike angels, he must rely on sacramental symbology, and he must struggle with ethics. In Stevens' transvaluations, the sacraments, as signs of spiritual reality and means to spiritual grace, become the evidence of imagination as it penetrates our social forms: "a ceremonious baptism, a ceremonious wedding, a ceremonious funeral," Stevens notes, "are instances" (NA 145). Social forms, however, are for Stevens less important than personal ceremonies, the intimate meetings and mergings of mind and world which he often celebrates and signifies through the Christian rites of marriage and communion. These sacraments, through a simple substitution of the earthly for the divine, figure for Stevens the moments of grace available to man through the processes of perception emerging in the poem or the aesthetic insight.

Stevens' ethics are, in a similar way, part of his aesthetics. Though he plays Pater in proclaiming "the morality of the poet's radiant and productive atmosphere" to be "the morality of the right sensation" (NA 58), Stevens is more like Arnold in the serious elaboration of his ethics. He too believed that "we have to turn to poetry to interpret life for us, to console us, to sustain us";[3] he believed that the poet's role is "to help people to live their lives" (NA 29). Sensation is perception, and perception, for Stevens, is everything. Therefore, the blessed are those who can see clearly, without evasion by nonsense, and feel strongly, without evasion by nostalgia. The "extreme poet" is the man who can do this and yet "be as concerned with a knowledge of man as people are now concerned with a knowledge of God." He is the poet who has "the knowledge of good and evil" (LWS 370).

Much of Stevens' ethics depends on his poetics: the rightness of the "right sensation" exists in the equilibrium of reality and imagination. If heaven is too much imagination and if hell, looking ominously like the twentieth century, is too much reality, paradise is the supreme integration, the perfect moment. The conclusion of Chapter Four, then, examines Stevens' personal salvation, the right integrations as he found them on the way from *Har-*

---

[3] Matthew Arnold, "The Study of Poetry" (1880), in *Poetry and Criticism of Matthew Arnold*, ed. A. Dwight Culler (Boston: Houghton Mifflin, 1961), p. 306.

monium to *The Rock*. Stevens believed, and he embodied this belief in his poems, that through the perception poetry commands we can accept "the health of the world" as "enough" (CP 315); in supreme moments, in "the ro-tund emotions . . . / The reverberating psalm, the right chorale" (CP 325-326), we can make our blood the blood of paradise.

~ 1 ~

LINEAGE AND LANGUAGE:
Stevens' Religious Heritage

> It is a habit of mind with me to be thinking of some
> substitute for religion. I don't necessarily mean some
> substitute for the church, because no one believes in
> the church as an institution more than I do. My
> trouble, and the trouble of a great many people, is
> the loss of belief in the sort of God in Whom we
> were all brought up to believe.
>
> (LWS 348)

WHAT Stevens confesses as a habit of mind, his poetry
and prose reveal to be a near obsession. His search for a
substitute for religion occupied his poetic energy from
the early poetry to the late. This energy vacillated between negative and positive poles, between condemnation
of the "deaf-mute churches" (CP 357) and affirmation of
personal, vital faith in "a chapel of breath" (CP 529).
These poles competed like powerful magnets so that his
contempt, though often jaunty, was rarely pure, because
he respected the church as a once omnipotent supreme
fiction, and his affirmations, though often rhapsodic, were
rarely total, because he feared the presumption of any
fiction which might call itself supreme. Stevens' heritage,
the piety of his ancestors the Zellers and of his own
youth, was belief in the sort of God Who joined the
visible and the invisible in symbol, rite, and creed. His
critique of religion in its twentieth-century dilapidation

9

rested on the assumption that new integrations, not wholly unlike the old, were possible. Stevens' momentary affirmations of such possible substitutes as the palace of art, romanticism, skepticism, naturalism, and humanism, however, were frail and tentative. His substitute is finally the search itself: poetry and the theory of poetry. The sort of God in Whom we can believe is imagination. His church is not the massively rigid cathedral but the chapel of breath: the personal, ephemeral, radiant, life-giving, and mutable merging of self and environment, visible and invisible.

"Winter Bells," the poem Stevens was explicating when he noted his habit of mind, is a listless poem arguing that "the strength of the church grows less and less until the church stands for little more than propriety" (LWS 348). It is a facile criticism, one Stevens had made many times before and would make again. The poem, included in *Ideas of Order* (1926), is striking, however, for its bleakness. Its negations lack the joviality of "A High-Toned Old Christian Woman," the savagery of "The Bird with the Coppery, Keen Claws," or the passion of "Sunday Morning." It has, unlike "Sunday Morning" or the later "Esthétique du Mal," no affirmations. It is a poem of exile. The Jew, who neither lives in his land nor speaks his language, does not go to the synagogue to be flogged but to the Catholic church to be exotically distracted:

> He preferred the brightness of bells,
> The *mille fiori* of vestments,
> The voice of centuries
> On the priestly gramophones.
>   (CP 141)

His "rage against chaos" is soothed by custom and stifled by tidy, irrelevant "regulations of his spirit." If puzzled, he promises himself to combat exile with exile, "to go to Florida one of these days" and "to give this further thought."

A true faith for Stevens is one vitally connected to our time, our land, and our language. In it we are at home in a place we know and a time we understand. There we live, Stevens explains in a pattern of speech that seems to comfort him, "as Danes in Denmark all day long" (CP 419); we absorb life "as the Angevine / Absorbs Anjou" (CP 224); our speech is "as the cackle of toucans / In the place of toucans" (CP 52); and our rituals, like those of Crispin's colonists, incorporate the peach and its incantations, the visible and the invisible. It is a blessing as well as a fatality that "all gods are created in the images of their creators" (OP 211), for if "God is a postulate of the ego" (OP 171), He is by that directly related to us, our land and our time. For the Irish, and not for the Jew, Catholicism is a true faith. "The identity of the Irish with their religion," Stevens remarked with some nostalgia, "is the same thing as the identity of the Irish with their lonely, misty, distant land, a Catholic country, breeding and fostering Catholic natures" (LWS 877). This is especially attractive to men living, like the Jew,

> in a place
> That is not our own and, much more, not ourselves
> And hard it is in spite of blazoned days.
> (CP 383)

We live without direct relation to either the visible, our land, or the invisible, our faith. For us, God is an abstraction; for the Irish, "in Ireland, God is a member of the family" (LWS 448).

Nearer, clearer, and more compelling than the winter bells for Stevens were "the old Lutheran bells at home" (CP 461), the bells that brought the intangible into the very tangible world of John Zeller, Stevens' maternal great-grandfather, a religious refugee who came to America in 1709 and settled in the Susquehanna Valley. In exile, he found a place his own and, much more, himself. The family house was, almost literally, a house of worship:

> Over the door there is an architectural cartouche of the cross with palm-branches below, placed there, no doubt, to indicate that the house and those that lived in it were consecrated to the glory of God. From this doorway they faced the hills that were part of the frame of their valley, the familiar shelter in which they spent their laborious lives, happy in the faith and worship in which they rejoiced. Their reality consisted of both the visible and the invisible.
>
> (NA 100)

Stevens' lingering description perhaps glances at Psalm 121: from the firm framework of their door, the Zellers would have contemplated the hills from whence came their help and the Lord who preserved their going out and coming in. Their life incorporated religious symbol, ritual, and faith as simply as it did the plough and hay-rake. Significantly, the Zellers remind Stevens of a "stout old Lutheran [who] felt about his church very much as the Irish are said to feel about God" (NA 100). More significantly, the Zellers are Stevens' blood, neither an abstraction nor an example but a living presence.

Stevens' poems about John Zeller stem from the quarrel between the great-grandfather and the skeptical realist in him: the one who "would sacrifice a great deal to be a Saint Augustine" and the other who replies, "but modernity is so Chicagoan, so plain, so unmeditative" (LWS 32). "The Bed of Old John Zeller" affirms the first of these competitors, "Two Versions of the Same Poem" the second. "The Bed of Old John Zeller" finds the poet, like the ephebe of "Notes toward a Supreme Fiction," tossing in bed. His is "voluble dumb violence" (CP 384): he cannot bellow like the lion, since he is alienated from his instinct, nor can he sing like the angel, since he is alienated from his spirit. He is not, however, alienated from old John Zeller, who lies within him as he lies within old John's bed. It is

> as if one's grandfather lay
> In one's heart and wished as he had always wished, unable
>
> To sleep in that bed for its disorder.
> (CP 327)

The poet is searching for an invisible structure of ideas which will fit and explain the visible, chaotic structure of things. Counting possible structures, "these ghostly sequences / Of the mind" (CP 326), as he might count sheep, the poet merely adds his "own disorder to disaster" and "makes more of it" (CP 326). This is, Stevens seems to feel, a fatal process. The structure of things without an explicating structure of ideas is chaos. Chaos produces despair, which in turn produces "the habit of wishing": nostalgia and self-delusion. In this process, the thinker inevitably loses touch with reality, falsifying the things of the earth as he progressively refines himself out of existence. At least, Stevens concludes, for old John Zeller, alienated from neither instinct nor spirit, "it was the structure / Of things . . . that was thought of in the old peak of night" (CP 327). Old John was at home in a religion which fused things and ideas, the visible and the invisible. Ideas had a tangible reality, so that the hills outside his door seemed to be the Lord who made and kept him.

In "Two Versions of the Same Poem," old John Zeller "stands / On his hill, watching the rising and falling" of the "human ocean" (CP 354). The sea is Stevens' customary image for chaos, the structure of things which defies any fixed structure of ideas. Like Crispin and the Doctor of Geneva, John Zeller confronts the sea and is at a loss. His structure of ideas, like Crispin's burgherhood and the Doctor of Geneva's Calvinism, is irrelevant. As if to emphasize old John's quaintness, Stevens makes him the exponent of a medieval theory. Zeller divides the mass into its elements—"sea, earth, sky—water // And fire and air"—and then, ineffectually, recognizes that "there is no golden solvent here" (CP 355). There is nothing quintessential, nothing that would be to the masses what John Zeller's faith was to him: an essence that permeated all nature and composed the heavens. Old John is as irrelevant to the world of *Owl's Clover* as the orderly old Pennsylvania Lutherans in "Dutch Graves in Bucks County" are to the turmoil of World War II. When Stevens addresses the Lutherans as "you, my semblables, whose ecstasy / Was the glory of heaven in the wilderness" (CP 292), the title is, as Joseph N. Riddel notes, "honorific yet ironic":[1] they are to be admired, perhaps even envied, but they will not be resurrected to deliver us from evil.

Stevens' pilgrimage to the Zeller home in September 1948 was part of his persistent and intense investigation of family origins. Genealogical research consumed much of Stevens' time, patience, and passion between the years 1942 and 1952, and it involved not only over four hundred dry and detailed letters remaining from this period but also the more lyric, if uncompleted, project for a Hymn to J. Zeller (LWS 792). Yet this pilgrimage to the Susquehanna Valley occurred as well in homage to Stevens' own youth. He was once, as the Zellers once were, "completely satisfied that behind every physical fact there is a divine force" (LWS 32). In Stevens' early letters and journals, it is difficult to sort the postured from the heartfelt, but two things are clear. He longed for the full, familial relationship with God and the land which the Zellers' faith had provided them, and he tended, at least during his New York years, to come alive only on Sundays. On Sundays, Stevens exercised his two principal forms of piety: homage to God in nature and homage to God in church. One Sunday in August 1902, after an hour in Saint Patrick's Cathedral and a seventeen-and-a-half mile walk—"a good day's jaunt"— Stevens contrasted his two deities: the presence in the cathedral and the presence on the highway. "The priest in me," he wrote, "worshipped one God at one shrine; the poet another God at another shrine. The priest wor-

[1] *The Clairvoyant Eye: The Poetry and Poetics of Wallace Stevens* (Baton Rouge: Louisiana State Univ. Press, 1965), p. 201.

shipped Mercy and Love; the Poet, Beauty and Might"
(LWS 59).

Mercy and Love appealed, Stevens confessed, in his
"more lonely moods" (LWS 58). In church he preferred
"dark corners . . . a great nave, quiet lights, a remote
voice, a soft choir and solitude" (LWS 86): a sensuous,
stimulating, yet isolating solace. He enjoyed hearing the
prayers of men and women and "dreaming with the
Congregation" (LWS 59), but his love and mercy were
vulnerable to fits of snobbish misanthropy. "Impossible
to be religious in a pew," he shuddered after one Sunday
in 1906. "Near me was a doddering girl of, say, twenty
—idiot eyes, spongy nose, shining cheeks." In her home-
made bonnet, she made him feel that "human qualities,
on an average, are fearful subjects for contemplation"
(LWS 86). Churches are "beautiful and full of comfort
and moral help," Stevens wrote his wife-to-be in 1907,
yet, he rather jauntily asserted, "they do not '*influence*'
any but the 'stupid' " (LWS 96).

If Stevens the skeptic is something of a dandy, Stevens
the jaunty woodland tramper sounds much like Emerson
and Whitman. A journal entry from 1899 is revealing.
First, Stevens, like Emerson finding particular natural
facts symbols of particular spiritual facts, affirms a divine
force behind every physical fact. Then, like Emerson,
he cautions himself not to "look *at* facts, but *through*
them." With a flourish reminiscent of Whitman, he signs
off "in this phrase alone: Salut au Monde!" (LWS 32-33).
Echoes of Emerson and Whitman, however, can be mis-
leading. Unlike the Transcendentalist, Stevens finds physical fact more enticing than divine force. His precise, loving descriptions of nature usually stop with sunset colors,
the sounds of rain, "the wet sides of leaves glitter[ing]

like plates of steel" (LWS 62). His intuitions of God seem more often a distraction than a passion. Sometimes they seem mere self-conscious conceit, as when, for instance, he noted that "stalks of golden rod burned in the shadows like flambeaux in my temple" (LWS 60-61). Stevens may have felt like Whitman when he "went tramping through the fields and woods [and] beheld every leaf and blade of grass revealing or rather betokening the Invisible" (LWS 59), but his Salut au Monde was not nearly as generous and expansive. He was, for example, revolted to find eggshells in the woods; they were, like the dingy girl in church, sure signs of humanity "loafing in my temple" (LWS 62).

Nature makes "a god of man," Stevens summarized, "but a chapel makes a man of him" (LWS 96). Neither was entirely satisfactory, and his attitude toward both lapsed easily into pose. But, he continually reaffirmed, "the feeling of piety is very dear to me" (LWS 32). "Piety" is a word Stevens never used in his poetry. When he uses it again in prose, it excludes the superfluous and defines his lasting concern. "I write poetry," he confessed in 1944, "because it is part of my piety" (LWS 473). His reverence was no longer for the action of God in nature. It involved instead the action of imagination in reality. It was not flippantly that in 1953, reprimanding an insistent scholar, he remarked, "I believe in pure explication de texte. This may in fact be my principal form of piety" (LWS 793). Poetry, or the imagination's explication of reality, became Stevens' piety.

The piety Stevens admitted in 1944 carries the emotional commitment of the piety he experienced in 1899, and, perhaps partly for that reason, when it emerges in his poetry it often assumes shapes traditionally given to the expression of religious piety. Stevens' use of biblical forms, symbols, and echoes is, like his search for a substitute for religion, a habit of mind. It evinces his desire, often difficult to tell from despair, to establish a poetic religion, one in which imagination replaces God as the prime mover. Stevens respected the church, and he wanted what it had provided the Zellers: a direct, encompassing relation with the visible and the invisible. The skeptic in him, however, knew reality had changed so thoroughly and violently that the old structure of ideas no longer fitted the new structure of things. His transmutation of the church's forms and symbols reveals his reverence for the accuracy that must admit a new structure of things. It also reveals his need for the old structure of ideas which the church had once embodied.

The major biblical forms that Stevens uses in his poetry are the parable, the proverb, the prayer, the hymn, and the psalm. The parable is usually defined as a brief narrative from which a moral can be drawn, but it differs from the short story or illustrative joke, also brief and pointed narratives, in several ways. First, and importantly, it is for us a specifically biblical form with a religious or ethical rather than a social or psychological aim. Although there are some Old Testament parables, the form is principally identified with Christ. The New Testament records forty-seven parables. They range from simple figurative statements, such as the comparison of the kingdom of God with a mustard seed (Mark 4.31), to more lengthy, involved, and developed narratives, such as the parable of the Good Samaritan (Luke 10.25-37), but each embodies a lesson to be learned by the faithful. Secondly, therefore, the intent is not primarily to amuse but to instruct. This has implications for the tone, since it distances the speaker from his audience. He is not a raconteur currying favor or an ancient mariner craving attention but a calm, detached teacher. This may involve some condescension, for the speaker's effort is to lead the unenlightened to an understanding of a difficult ethical situation through a comparison with a more simple, earthy, familiar situation. It may also involve some elitism, since inevitably the audience divides into the sheep who comprehend and the goats who do not, and perhaps cannot. Christ, explaining his method to the disciples, distinguishes between their knowledge and that of the masses: "It is given unto you to know the mysteries of the kingdom of heaven, but to them it is not given.... Therefore speak I to them in parables: because they seeing, see not; and hearing, they hear not, neither do they understand" (Matthew 13.11,13). The burden of penetrating the mystery is on the audience rather than on the narrator: in the Old Testament, God commands and men obey; in the New Testament, Christ hints and men ponder. Finally, as a result of its structure, the parable is what Stevens terms one of the "effects of analogy" (NA 105). It demands the pondering of parallels. For this reason, it may, but need not, be an allegory in which each character or object stands for an abstraction otherwise hard to grasp. The danger here is that, as Stevens points out with reference to Bunyan, "the other meaning divides our attention and this diminishes our enjoyment of the story." The ideal which he sought in his parables was the conjunction of concrete and abstract: "the story and the other meaning should come together like two aspects that combine to produce a third or, if they do not combine, inter-act, so that one influences the other and produces an effect similar in kind to the prismatic formations that occur about us in nature" (NA 109). Stevens' parables are always doctrinal, sometimes condescending and elitist, and usually intricate in their analogy, but they are always a fusion of the concrete and the abstract, the visible and the invisible.

As in his work with other biblical patterns, Stevens adapts the parable to his own ends. Often he designs his own parables with symbolically named characters, such as Cotton and black Sly (CP 126) or Nanzia Nunzio and Ozymandias (CP 395), but sometimes he converts the pre-established outlines of Christ's parables into illustrations of his own doctrine. His revisions of the parables of the Prodigal Son and the Ten Virgins are interesting and complex examples of the way in which Stevens adapted Christian patterns to his poetic beliefs.

Christ's parable of the Prodigal Son (Luke 15.11-32) demonstrates God's delight in receiving the repentant sinner. Section II of Stevens' "Certain Phenomena of Sound" takes its outlines:

So you're home again, Redwood Roamer, and ready
To feast . . . Slice the mango, Naaman, and dress it

With white wine, sugar and lime juice. Then bring it,
After we've drunk the Moselle, to the thickest shade

Of the garden. We must prepare to hear the Roamer's
Story.

(CP 286)

The Roamer's wanderings remain vague: he might be the alienated cynic of "Palace of the Babies," Adam outside Eden, any man in a place not his own. The presence in his name of "red," a color which Stevens frequently uses to imply reality, hints that he has been enmeshed, like the Prodigal Son, in things as they are. As he moves from the sun into the shade, he returns to the harmony Stevens cherishes: home, the feast in the garden, poetry. His salvation is the speaking of his "most prolific narrative" (CP 287), a sign and symbol of his reconciliation with imagination.

Stevens' rewriting of the parable of the Ten Virgins (Matthew 25.1-13) is more complicated. The biblical parable stresses the necessity to prepare for the kingdom of heaven. Christ the bridegroom, it assures us, will come to deliver the faithful. Stevens' "Ghosts as Cocoons," written in 1936, is a plea for delivery. It expresses, Stevens explains, a "profound desire to be released from all our misfortunes" (LWS 347). The poem is a double reversal of the parable. First, it is not the bridegroom but the bride that is supplicated:

Come now. Those to be born have need

Of the bride, love being a birth, have need to see
And to touch her.
      (CP 119)

She must come to the "butcher, seducer, bloodman, reveller" (CP 119): the inept politicians, the evil and unhappiness of the Depression (LWS 347). Reality for Stevens is usually masculine, and the reality of the Depression was defiantly and unpleasantly so.

The love and birth brought to the marriage is, in the Bible, Christian faithfulness and final ascension into the kingdom of heaven. The one involves and implies the other as reward. For Stevens these become imagination and the cyclical movement into spring, the glorious but tentative beginnings of a process inextricably intertwined with the most natural of deaths and resurrections. Stevens' bride is literally spring, the "pearled and pasted, bloomy-leafed" deliverer (CP 119) come to lead us into a purely natural, simply fulfilling kingdom of earth, yet the rebirth of reality involves and implies for Stevens the rebirth of imagination and therefore the bride has also a figurative meaning. If winter is the triumph of reality's starkness, spring, as Frank Kermode points out, is Stevens' "analogue of the mind's producing 'what will suffice' to clothe the intolerable body of reality."[2] Spring brings a spiritual as well as a physical rebirth, and the bride is thus a figure like the muse of such poems as "To the One of Fictive Music": a sign of the imagination which alone provides a structure of ideas for the intolerable structure of things. Earth has made its preparations, Stevens emphasizes: "The grass is in seed. The young birds are flying. . . . / / The vetch has turned purple. But where," he asks, "is the bride?" (CP 119). Until she arrives we are as ghosts awaiting ascension into spring, chrysalises in cocoons waiting for wings.

"Ghosts as Cocoons" and Section II of "Certain Phenomena of Sound" are parables in their biblical tone, instructive aim, and fusion of concrete narrative particulars with abstract ethical implications. Stevens adapted Christ's parables with ease because their pattern was part of his heritage and habit of mind, but he did not always rely on Christ for the plot. He relished the fashioning of his own parables: some bizarre and unorthodox, others more traditional.

[2] *Wallace Stevens* (New York: Grove Press, 1961), p. 35.

Stevens' favored form, the anecdote, is a sly twist of the parable. The word "anecdote" is from the Greek *anekdota*, meaning unpublished items, usually historical or biographical. Unlike the parable, which is a sophisticated, stylized fabrication in illustration of a moral lesson, the anecdote is traditionally a simple, factual account of an episode inherently entertaining. Whereas the parable is true in its fiction, the anecdote is supposed to be true in its facts; whereas the one is produced by imagination, the other is a product of reality. For Stevens, however, there are no convenient and clear-cut distinctions between fact and fiction or between reality and imagination, and he takes a perverse joy in blending anecdote and parable. "Earthy Anecdote," "Anecdotal Revery," "Anecdote of Men by the Thousand," "Anecdote of Canna," "Anecdote of the Prince of Peacocks," "Anecdote of the Abnormal," and "Anecdote of the Jar" are tall tales, as extravagant as anecdotes about Davy Crockett. Dealing with such things as firecats, the red prince Berserk, and the huge canna in the dreams of X, they cannot be mistaken for fact but are parables as they might be told on the frontier: fictions posing, through Stevens' sleight-of-hand, as fact.

The anecdotes, often allegorical, are parabolic in construction and intent. Usually, like the parable, they juxtapose estranged forces, for as the parables contrast the heavenly bridegroom and earthly virgin, the forgiving father and exiled son, Stevens' anecdotes, John J. Enck summarizes, "turn upon diametric poles like reality-illusion, art-nature, waking-sleep, tangible-transcendent."[3] Both parable and anecdote end in reconciliation: the

[3] *Wallace Stevens: Images and Judgments* (Carbondale: Southern Illinois Univ. Press, 1964), p. 55.

marriage, the feast, the compromise, or the sudden, surprising merger of opposites. The reconciliation is, aptly enough in an anecdotal parable, a blending of the imagined and the real: the firecat and the bucks, the canna in X's dream and the canna on his terrace, the dread of the bushy plain which Berserk roams and the beauty of the moonlight falling there.

"A Rabbit as King of the Ghosts" is a more traditional parable and a particularly good example of Stevens' usual parabolic method. Like other of the parables, it contrasts reality and illusion, here warning, like a Christian parable, against complacency. We must be realists of the imagination; we must beware of the dangers of false imagination, of sentimentality and wish fulfillment. The rabbit represents the self-delusive ego. Though it is insignificant, though its enemy the cat is in the grass, it yields luxuriously to solipsism: it becomes "a self that fills the four corners of night. / The red cat hides away in the fur-light" (CP 209). Imagination which distorts things as they are imperils life. Like Bunyan's Christian, Stevens' imaginative man is beset with danger. To yield to falsifying wish fulfillment, the parable emphasizes, is death.

The proverb is often the distillation of a parable, and Stevens moved easily between parable and proverb, illustration and aphorism. The proverb, a pithy statement alleging a truth, often preceded its poetic elaboration for Stevens. Unlike his friendly rival William Carlos Williams, who found "no ideas but in things,"[4] Stevens seems first to come upon the idea, then to incarnate it in things. The poem "Theory" begins with the aphorism "I

[4] *Paterson* (New York: New Directions, 1963), p. 14.

am what is around me" (cp 86), gives three of a possibly
infinite series of examples, and concludes, "These are
merely instances" (cp 87). Three facts from Samuel
French Morse's "Introduction" to *Opus Posthumous*
hint that this is a paradigm of the way Stevens habitually
worked. One of Stevens' notebooks, the "Adagia," is
filled with aphorisms which reappear entire in his poems
and prose. It is, Morse comments, Stevens' "book of
proverbs."[5] Another notebook, "From Pieces of Paper,"
contains titles for poems. These often are indistinguish-
able, except by capitalization, from proverbs: for example, "One Must Sit Still to Discover the World,"
"Reality Is an Activity of the Most August Imagination,"
"The Ultimate Poem is Abstract." Finally, he seems to
have relied on aphorism to organize his long poems.
Stevens' outline for "Abecedarium of Finesoldier" (op
xxiv) is the only outline remaining among his notes. A
late project, the poem was presumably planned as a companion to "Examination of the Hero in a Time of War"
or "Esthétique du Mal." Stevens' outline for it, probably
typical of preparations for the long poems which preceded and followed it, consists of ten statements, one for
each projected section. Five of them are as abstract and
aphoristic as the heading for Section IV: "Invisible fate
becomes visible" (op xxiv). Stevens' tendency to think
in proverbs is a habit of mind, an inheritance from the
Zellers and from his early religious training. The statement of equivalence verging on axiom—a statement like
"God and the imagination are one" (cp 524)—is, Frank
Doggett notes, a major feature of Stevens' style, "a bur-
geoning from the moralizing strain in Colonial literature

---

[5] "Introduction," p. xxxi.

with its reliance on the Bible and the popular maxim."[6]

A proverb may be as secular as Poor Richard, but a prayer, by definition, is an approach to God in word or thought. Prayer was a form that haunted Stevens. It posed special problems for a nonbeliever, however, and Stevens solved these in several ways. "Flyer's Fall," a poem of World War II, is a prayer to the absence of God. "Receive" in the Bible indicates ascension: Christ was "received" into heaven (Acts 1.9), the Psalmist knows God shall "receive" him (Psalm 49.15). In prayer it requests afterlife, and Stevens uses it in prayer for the fallen flyer, a prayer to the nonbeing of after-death:

> Darkness, nothingness of human after-death,
> Receive and keep him in the deepnesses of space—
>
> Profundum, physical thunder, dimension in which
> We believe without belief, beyond belief.
>
> (CP 336)

The flyer's fall is, paradoxically, an ascension into the depths of space. The God traditional prayer addresses and the "nothingness" Stevens addresses are alike fictive. We can believe in them without belief because, as Stevens explains in "Asides on the Oboe," "final belief / Must be in a fiction" (CP 250), one we trust but also one we know we have ourselves created.

The imagination is the creator of the fictive, the origin of belief. It is the power Stevens most often addresses in prayer. The rhythms of prayer seem to preoccupy Stevens, perhaps because he felt the similarity between

[6] "Wallace Stevens' Later Poetry," *ELH*, 25 (June 1958), 146.

poetry and prayer. "Poetry," he noted in the "Adagia," "is like prayer in that it is most effective in solitude and in the times of solitude as, for example, in the earliest morning" (OP 163). These rhythms emerge even in the singsong plea of "Sailing after Lunch":

> Mon Dieu, hear the poet's prayer.
> The romantic should be here.
> The romantic should be there.
>
> (CP 120)

Stevens, like the Weeping Burgher, distorts with a certain malice (CP 61). The rhythm of prayer, markedly seductive to him, here collapses into the rhythm of nursery rhyme to parody the puerility of wish-fulfilling sentimentalists and perhaps also to mock his own attraction toward a form which, in its traditional use, he could only discard.

Stevens feels a similar mixture of attraction and revulsion for the most intense of all prayers, the incantatory and supplicating litany. The first two lines of "Le Monocle de Mon Oncle," for example—lines which read "Mother of heaven, regina of the clouds, / O sceptre of the sun, crown of the moon" (CP 13)—are an indulgence Stevens seems to enjoy but one which he immediately and gleefully deflates in the next two lines. Richard Ellmann emphasizes that "the first two lines, which echo the litany, are pseudo-religious."[7] They are satiric. In "To the One of Fictive Music," on the other hand, Stevens indulges himself freely:

[7] "Wallace Stevens' Ice-Cream," *Kenyon Review*, 19 (Winter 1957), 97.

Sister and mother and diviner love,
And of the sisterhood of the living dead
Most near, most clear, and of the clearest bloom,
And of the fragrant mothers the most dear
And queen, and of diviner love the day
And flame and summer and sweet fire, no thread
Of cloudy silver sprinkles in your gown
Its venom of renown, and on your head
No crown is simpler than the simple hair.

(CP 87)

Enck notes in these lines "all the trademarks of a pseudo-Biblical incantation, the repeated words (*and* 11 times in 9 lines) and rhymes which stumble over each other."[8] The One of Fictive Music is the muse of imagination, the intercessor between the mind and reality. She is the sister in the sisterhood of the muses, the "diviner love" Stevens calls our "interior paramour" (CP 524), the mother at the creative source of our being. We pray to her because she helps us live our lives at a time when, for most of us, religious sanctions are no longer relevant. The One of Fictive Music is for Stevens the sole power to deserve the dignity and intensity of human prayer.

Hymns and psalms are the fictive music of religion, made in praise and worship of God. Stevens, Frank Lentricchia comments, "uses the hymn to figure the poem in a number of places, and . . . he wants us to keep the religious context in mind." This is not, however, as Lentricchia would have it, because we are to think of the hymn as a "glorious self-delusion of the imagination."[9]

[8] *Images and Judgments*, p. 73.
[9] *The Gaiety of Language: An Essay on the Radical Poetics of*

Like the parable, proverb, and prayer, the hymn retains its religious form and emotion while Stevens turns its content toward things of this world. The secular glory of supple, brilliant freshness, "the world of a moment" in "Polo Ponies Practicing," is, Stevens affirms, "fitted . . . / For hymns" (OP 37). Stevens' "Reply to Papini" defends these "humane triumphals" (CP 447) against Pope Celestin VI's demand for "the hymn of victory or the psalm of supplication" (CP 446). The humane hymns are tentative yet heroic because they share the confusions of intelligence which faith denies:

> These are hymns appropriate to
> The complexities of the world, when apprehended,
>
> The intricacies of appearance, when perceived.
> They become our gradual possession.
>   (CP 447)

"Notes toward a Supreme Fiction" returns to this theme: to repeat the old hymns is "a facile exercise"; to catch and celebrate the ever-changing new is "the difficultest rigor" (CP 398).

Stevens' poems, it sometimes seems, comprise a revised hymnal. Several critics have noted that *Harmonium*, Stevens' first volume of verse, is named for a small parlor organ used in family hymn singing.[10] Its thesis is that, as

---

W. B. Yeats and Wallace Stevens (Berkeley: Univ. of California Press, 1968), p. 160.

[10] See, among others, Enck, *Images and Judgments*, p. 46, and Geoffrey Moore, "Wallace Stevens: A Hero of Our Time," in *The Great Experiment in American Literature*, ed. Carl Bode

the poet tells the woman of "Sunday Morning," divinity lives within the human realm. In its poems, Stevens searches for "bravura adequate to this great hymn" (CP 16): like Crispin, he takes "the vulgar, as his theme and hymn and flight" (CP 35); he writes an elegant "Hymn from a Watermelon Pavilion" (CP 88); he responds to Florida with casual, spontaneous "hymn and hymn" (CP 95). This aim reappears in the later poems: in the "Late Hymn from the Myrrh-Mountain" (CP 349), written perhaps with the biblical mountain of myrrh (Song of Solomon 4.6) in mind, in Stevens' "Night-Hymn" to the rock (CP 528), and in the "hero-hymns," "day hymns," and "hymns of the struggle of the idea of god" (CP 185), the "calendar hymn" (CP 382), "imagination's hymns" (CP 439), and "marriage-hymns" (CP 373) which fill his work. Even Ananke, the severe serpent god of "The Greenest Continent," has "his hymn, his psalm, his cithern song of praise" (OP 59).

The psalm, a sacred song or poem in praise of God, is a hymn raised to the power of the biblical hymns collected in the Book of Psalms. It is appropriate to the intensest moments, moments when

> The green corn gleams and the metaphysicals
> Lie sprawling in majors of the August heat,
> The rotund emotions, paradise unknown.
> This is the thesis scrivened in delight,
> The reverberating psalm, the right chorale.
>   (CP 325-326)

(New York: Frederick A. Praeger, 1961), rpt. in *The Achievement of Wallace Stevens*, ed. Ashley Brown and Robert S. Haller (New York: J. B. Lippincott, 1962), p. 252.

The hymn, the song of praise, the reverberating psalm affirm life. To sustain them, to compose a hymnal or book of psalms, would be evidence that the rotund emotions in their recurrence are enough. In "The Man with the Blue Guitar" Stevens demands just this from himself: "a poem like a missal found / In the mud" (CP 177). A missal is a concentrated hymnal: a book containing all that is said or sung in the mass for the entire year. "I desire my poem," Stevens commented, "to mean as much, and as deeply, as a missal. While I am writing what appear to be trifles, I intend these trifles to be a missal for brooding-sight: for an understanding of the world" (LWS 790).

Stevens' trifles aim at no less than apotheosis. "Apotheosis," Louis L. Martz explains, "elevates the mortal to the stature of divinity; it glorifies; and the appropriate poetry of apotheosis is therefore the hymn, the ode, the celebration, the chant."[11] Apotheosis is Stevens' purpose

---

[11] "Wallace Stevens: The World as Meditation," *Yale Review*, n.s., 47 (Summer 1958), rpt. in *Wallace Stevens: A Collection of Critical Essays*, ed. Marie Borroff (Englewood Cliffs, N.J.: Prentice-Hall, 1963), p. 143. Stevens' poetry, Martz argues, has a place in the tradition of formal religious meditation, as practiced by men like Herbert, Donne, and Hopkins. The highly formalized process of religious meditation is threefold: composition of place, presentation and analysis of a problem, and resolution in a spirit of devotion. Martz's discussion presents two problems: was Stevens' use of the form consciously traditional? If not, if Stevens discovered it independently, why, as a modern poet vastly different in knowledge and belief from the seventeenth-century meditative poets, did he find it congenial? At Harvard, Stevens took courses in the literature of the eighteenth and nineteenth centuries, but he had no more specific study of the seventeenth century than might be offered in a course like "History and Development of English Literature in outline"

in most of his work with traditional religious forms. His transvaluations of parable, proverb, prayer, and hymn are efforts to create a new religion. They defer to the supreme integrations of the old by retaining the vocabulary and purpose; they acknowledge new realities by changing the content.

Stevens' use of biblical symbol is a further, more intense indication that religious thought informs his work. He attempts to make his symbols work as religious symbols worked, and he amplifies his own symbols by selective use of biblical referents. "Symbol," from the Greek *symballein*—to throw together—signifies the merging of two worlds: the world of commonplace objects and the otherwise invisible world of essences, values, and intangibles. Using Ecclesiastes as an example, Stevens in "Three Academic Pieces" explains that images are not "the language of reality," mere denotative reference to commonplace objects. They are "the symbolic language of metamorphosis, or resemblance, of poetry": connotative, expansive reference. Through resemblance, images tie the two worlds: they "relate to reality and they intensify our sense of it and they give us the pleasure of 'lentor and solemnity' in respect to the most commonplace ob-

---

(LWS 17). There is no mention of Donne or Herbert in Stevens' letters and essays. Martz suggests that Stevens happened on the form by affinity, so that "an analogous situation called forth the analogous discipline" (Martz, p. 145). Stevens' psychological need for a modern substitute for religion generated forms both unconsciously and consciously religious. Martz deals with the seemingly unconscious appearance of a meditative process which relates Stevens to a tradition of explicitly religious poetry; I am concerned with Stevens' development of a unique and complex system which employs traditional religious forms, values, and beliefs to create a religion of poetry.

jects" (NA 78). Through this process, for example, the symbol of the hills, to the Christian who holds that concrete phenomena manifest another world, reveals aspects of God otherwise inexpressible. Symbol, by definition, accomplishes for the modern poet what religion accomplished for the Zellers and for the Irish: it unites the visible and the invisible.

Stevens was not, as Michel Benamou[12] has shown, a strict symboliste. Though he was influenced by Valéry and Mallarmé, he rejected the extreme form of symbolisme which involved a search for an ideal world beyond reality and a system of correspondences dependent on a pure, refined, and inaccessible realm. Where the symboliste aesthetic often demanded that the poet spurn the physical world, Stevens' aesthetic always required that the man of imagination celebrate, refresh, and restore reality. Nor, except for a brief flirtation in *Owl's Clover*, was Stevens a believer in the collective unconscious as a repository of symbols. He did attempt to build a coherent symbolic system, a system as thorough as any biblical exegete might ask. Many critics have assumed that Stevens' symbols are on the whole private and constant, so that blue, for example, always indicates imagination, green reality, black death, and so on. Though this assumption has its dangers, it seems largely

[12] See *Wallace Stevens and the Symbolist Imagination* (Princeton: Princeton Univ. Press, 1972) and "Beyond Emerald or Amethyst: Wallace Stevens and the French Tradition," *Dartmouth College Library Bulletin*, n.s., 4 (December 1961), 60-66. For an opposing view, see Haskell M. Block, "The Impact of French Symbolism on Modern American Poetry," in *The Shaken Realist: Essays in Modern Literature in Honor of Frederick J. Hoffman*, ed. Melvin J. Friedman and John B. Vickery (Baton Rouge: Louisiana State Univ. Press, 1970), pp. 165-217.

accurate. But Stevens' symbolic system is not only self-referent. He also builds on references to other symbolic systems, among them biblical symbolism. His use of biblical symbol, like his use of biblical form, shows Stevens' need for religious integrations no longer viable. Reference to a biblical symbol can often clarify an otherwise enigmatic passage, since Stevens, though he may change the stress, rarely alters the manifest content of the symbol. Symbols like the rainbow, the dove, the prophet's star, and the burning bush appear in his poetry with an emphasis and meaning parallel to those of their biblical counterparts. The two most revealing examples of his appropriation of biblical symbol, however, are his symbolic usages of grass and glass.

In the Bible, grass often signifies the transience of mortal life: "All flesh is as grass, and all the glory of man as the flower of grass. The grass withereth, and the flower thereof falleth away" (I Peter 1.24; see also Isaiah 40.6-8). The biblical stress, that unlike grass "the word of the Lord endureth for ever" (I Peter 1.25), shifts in "Sunday Morning" to Stevens' stress:

> There is not any haunt of prophecy,
> Nor any old chimera of the grave . . .
> Nor visionary south, nor cloudy palm
> Remote on heaven's hill, that has endured
> As April's green endures.
>   (CP 68)

In "Ghosts as Cocoons" Stevens transforms the apocalyptic arrival of Christ into the cyclical arrival of the bride as spring. Here again, what in the Bible is linear is for Stevens cyclical. Like the bride, April's green comes every spring, and it endures beyond any abstraction from it. "The wheel," as Stevens explains in "The Sense of the Sleight-of-Hand Man," "survives the myths" (CP 222).

After this knowledge, however, we still, like the woman of "Sunday Morning," must consider death. Easily, traditionally, the image of flesh as grass links with the figure of death as the grim reaper who comes at apocalypse to mow the grass (Revelation 14.15). Two of Stevens' poems draw from this biblical source. In "Two at Norfolk" the images of grass and the reaper merge with a third, that of death as the black man, in Stevens' opening command: "Mow the grass in the cemetery, darkies" (CP 111). The poem emphasizes the continuance of life in defiance of death and darkness. The son and daughter of the dead, Jamanda and Carlotta, meet to make love on the graves of their fathers; they flourish as new flowers from old. The reaper's function is not to obliterate the old but to ensure the new: "Make a bed," the poet asks death in the last line, "and leave the iris in it" (CP 112).

"Esthétique du Mal" is a less high-handed effort to construct an ethic congruent with mortality, and it contains a more puzzling reference. A scene of apocalyptic devastation begins, "At dawn, / The paratroopers fall and as they fall / They mow the lawn" (CP 322). This may seem a surrealist trick not much different from Stevens' caricature of the surrealist image: "to make a clam play an accordion" (OP 177). It is actually biblical recasting. The paratroopers, who resemble the angels sighting machine guns in *Owl's Clover* (OP 56), are the new angels of death falling from the sky to reap their grim harvest of flesh.

The symbol of grass may have engaged Stevens because it involves mortality, a concern central to his thinking. The image of glass touches another of Stevens' favorite topics: sight. Saint Paul uses it to figure the cleared perspective which will include the heavenly with the earthly: "For now we see through a glass, darkly; but then face to face: now I know in part; but then shall I know even as also I am known" (I Corinthians 13.12). Our fallen nature, Saint Paul means, obscures our sight, so that now we see only the effect, not the cause, only the temporal not the eternal, the visible not the invisible. Section VI of "Thirteen Ways of Looking at a Blackbird" seems to incorporate this idea:

> Icicles filled the long window
> With barbaric glass.
> The shadow of the blackbird
> Crossed it, to and fro.
> The mood
> Traced in the shadow
> An indecipherable cause.
> (CP 93)

As icicles obscure a window, nature blocks perception, emotions thwart right reason. "Stevens' man, like St. Paul," Peter L. McNamara points out, "sees the shadow of reality, but loses sight of the object which produces it."[13] For both Saint Paul and Stevens, we know truth only through its refraction in reality. We see only in part.

[13] "The Multi-Faceted Blackbird and Wallace Stevens' Poetic Vision," *College English*, 25 (March 1964), 447.

Saint Paul's image is easily understood if "glass" is taken to mean a translucent pane, as in a window, but this reading is doubtful. The Vulgate translates the word as *speculum*, or mirror. This translation may have attracted Stevens, since its implications fit his theory of perception. If, in our fallen state, we see as in a mirror, we apprehend only ourselves reflected. Reality then is not things as they are but things as we are. To clear our sight, we must see beyond ourselves, for only if we efface ourselves as far as humanly possible can we see reality face to face. This twist of meaning is characteristic of Stevens: what is turned to heaven in biblical form or symbol is turned to earth in Stevens' transvaluation.

Stevens' poetry is full of narcissists who see into reality as into a mirror. This, Stevens feels, is our heritage from Eve. Eve in Eden

> made air the mirror of herself,

> Of her sons and of her daughters. They found them-
>   selves
> In heaven as in a glass.
> (cp 383)

This habit of perception is seductive but damning; through it, we further isolate ourselves from a reality quite definitely not in our image. The Franciscan don of "The Man with the Blue Guitar" recreates Eve's fall. His creed is made of "masks," facets of himself projected onto the world and rigidified there. In this,

> The shapes are wrong and the sounds are false.
> The bells are the bellowing of bulls.

> Yet Franciscan don was never more
> Himself than in this fertile glass.
>
> (CP 181)

This method of thought is comforting, but it is a betrayal of reality and of ourselves. It is an obscuring of sight.

From these considerations derives Stevens' third use of "glass": a transparency which allows us to escape the pathetic fallacy and to see as wholly as it is possible for us to see. Stevens' hero, "the impossible possible philosophers' man" (CP 250), is "the man of glass . . . the transparence of the place in which / He is" (CP 250-251). His is winter sight,[14] when all the mind's projections onto reality disappear and reality in all its bareness is exposed. This process, as Section xxx of "An Ordinary Evening in New Haven" explains,

> is a coming on and a coming forth.
> The pines that were fans and fragrances emerge,
> Staked solidly in a gusty grappling with rocks.
>
> The glass of the air becomes an element—
> It was something imagined that has been washed away.
> A clearness has returned. It stands restored.
>
> (CP 487-488)

This is a culmination of Stevens' use of the biblical image. The poem, as Helen Vendler observes, "becomes . . . beatific vision, as Stevens continues with a variation on Saint Paul: no longer are we making rubbings on a glass

---

[14] Thus he is also termed "a shell of . . . ice" (CP 297). For the significance of winter in Stevens' symbology, see Kermode, p. 34.

through which we peer; the whole glass is suddenly transparent, and thought, that skeleton in our flesh, is suddenly as clear as the skeletal tree trunks. It is a moment of pure reason."[15] The returned clarity is purified perception. The man of imagination achieves this radiance through poetry or poetic perception just as Saint Paul's man would achieve it through God. The resultant state of blessedness is a restoration to an almost prelapsarian oneness with the visible and the invisible.

Biblical forms and symbols were a general heritage for most men of Stevens' generation. The parable and proverb, and, more rarely, the hymn and prayer, can be forms of secular as well as religious literature, and biblical symbols may occur as readily to the lay as to the clerical mind. But in Stevens' work they recur so frequently and in such moments of intensity that they amount to a habit of mind. They are part of Stevens' search for a substitute for religion, and, as such, they convey a religious resonance as intense as that they bore for earlier generations. This habit of mind extends into Stevens' use of language, a use which includes biblical quotation, rhythm, words, and phrasing.

Several critics have noted a general biblical quality to Stevens' writing, especially in the penultimate stanza of "Sunday Morning" which Fuchs and Cunningham, among others, single out for its biblical phrasing.[16] The letters, particularly those of the early years, show that this quality is no accident. Stevens knew, and remembered

[15] *On Extended Wings: Wallace Stevens' Longer Poems* (Cambridge, Mass.: Harvard Univ. Press, 1969), p. 296.

[16] Daniel Fuchs, *The Comic Spirit of Wallace Stevens* (Durham, N.C.: Duke Univ. Press, 1963), p. 189; Cunningham, *Tradition and Poetic Structure*, p. 120.

in moments of nostalgia and bewilderment, many biblical passages. "I wish," he sighed in his journal in 1906,
"that groves still *were* sacred—or, at least, that something
was: that there was still something free from doubt, that
day unto day still uttered speech, and night unto night
still showed wisdom" (LWS 86). This slightly misquoted
rendering of Psalm 19.2 ("Day unto day uttereth speech,
and night unto night sheweth knowledge") is uneasy and
self-conscious: biblical quotation was comforting, but it
was also unsettling to Stevens' skeptical side. Again in
1923, in a letter to his wife from Greensboro, North
Carolina, Stevens admitted that in poverty and despair he
"might well depend on some such potent illusion as 'The
eternal God is thy refuge' [Deut. 33.27]," but he redeems
this momentary lapse with a description of the towns-
people for whom God is a refuge: they are "physically
weak and imperfect . . . mentally almost as bad" (LWS
237)—not quite imbeciles, he adds charitably, but not insurance executives from the Northeast either.

Stevens feels more comfortable quoting scripture in his
essays, perhaps because formal prose permits distance,
perhaps because in context any sentimentality is negated
by mischief or self-conscious blasphemy, perhaps because
by the 1940s when Stevens began to write essays his religious feelings had transferred from the church to poetry. In "The Figure of the Youth as Virile Poet" (1943),
arguing that poets are "the peers of saints," Stevens implies that poetry is "a vocation so that all men may know
the truth and that the truth may set them free" (NA 51).
This is a biblical passage (John 8.32) which intrigues
Stevens, though he prefers to use it paradoxically. Poetry
is the search for truth, and the search, ironically, frees us
from *the* truth—from any rigidified dogma. "The Latest

Freed Man," a poem from *Parts of a World* (1942), describes the moment of poetic animation in which the hero is free because he has "just / Escaped from the truth" (CP 204). This poem joins with the two preceding—"The Man on the Dump" and "On the Road Home"—to recast scripture: men must reject *the* truth ("the the" [CP 203]), for rejection of the truth sets men free. The youth as virile poet embodies the search which is poetry, just as Christ embodies the truth which is God. Thus he can proclaim, allowing Stevens a final scriptural quotation and blasphemy, "*I am the truth*" (NA 63).

Stevens' poetry, like his prose, consciously incorporates biblical wording and echo. The style is elastic enough to absorb recondite allusion, portmanteau words, schoolboy Latin, Jacobean pun, and French phrasing, but certain biblical terms often stand out rather awkwardly. That they are awkward and that Stevens, despite his meticulous ear, nevertheless enjoyed employing them indicates that these terms held a special fascination for him. The effect can seem gratuitous, or even ridiculous. "Behold," used as in scriptural injunction, appears in "Invective against Swans," "A Thought Revolved," and "Extracts from Addresses to the Academy of Fine Ideas," usually to introduce an aphoristic solemnity or portentous example. Echo of the formulaic "begat" occurs playfully in "The Sail of Ulysses," which speaks of "the John-begat-Jacob of what we know" (OP 103), and satirically in "Notes toward a Supreme Fiction," which has Jerome, through his translation of the Bible, beget "the tubas and the fire-wind strings" (CP 398) of our facile religious celebrations. More puzzling is the phrase, from "The Dove in the Belly," "Selah, tempestuous bird" (CP 366). "Selah," used in Psalms and Habakkuk, is thought to be a solemn exclamation or a musical direction. Here, employed mainly for atmospheric effect, it intrudes.

Scriptural phrasing comes most naturally to Stevens for two very specific effects: satiric deflation of religious cliché or serious elevation of the mortal to the divine. "Phases," one of Stevens' earliest published poems, contains an example of the first effect, a witty reversal and deflation of I Corinthians 15.55: "O death, where is thy sting? O grave, where is thy victory?" In the Bible, of course, heaven negates the sting with its victory over mortality. In a world without heaven to follow, luckless Fallen Winkle suffers, succinctly, death's "short, triumphant sting" (OP 5).

Stevens' serious use of biblical echo is almost always to attribute to the imagination the powers and prerogatives of God. "The Auroras of Autumn" VII rephrases Psalm 19 to make the "heavens . . . proclaim" (CP 417) the imagination enthroned in the firmament. The imaginative man in "Re-statement of Romance" echoes God's "I AM THAT I AM" (Exodus 3.14) in asserting, "I am what I am" (CP 146). "Puella Parvula," a late poem, sounds the poet's *"summarium in excelsis"* (CP 456), a phrase which, as Marie Borroff explains, alludes to "such biblical phrases as 'hosanna in excelsis' and 'gloria in excelsis' " and "implies that the revealed truth of imaginative vitality can fully compensate for the lost truth of religious revelation."[17]

One phrase which especially haunted Stevens was the divine fiat: "And God said, Let there be light: and there was light" (Genesis 1.3). Stevens' "echo to the great trumpet-call of 'Let there be light,' " Northrop Frye

[17] "Wallace Stevens: The World and the Poet," in *Critical Essays*, ed. Borroff, p. 21.

writes, "is 'All things in the sun are sun,' "[18] but there are other, more direct echoes. "He called hydrangeas purple," "Anecdote of the Abnormal" begins, "And they were" (op 23). "Thou art not August," the poet-hero of "Asides on the Oboe" proclaims, "unless I make thee so" (cp 251). The theory behind such statements is most fully elaborated in "Description without Place." If things exist in our perception of them, then what a thing seems it is: to seem is to be. What a thing seems is signified by the name (description) we give it; therefore, naming is creating. The poet, who has the power of naming, creates seeming and, therefore, like God, creates being:

> Thus the theory of description matters most.
> It is the theory of the word for those
>
> For whom the word is the making of the world,
> The buzzing world and lisping firmament.
>
> (cp 345)

In this poem the green queen of Section 1 exemplifies imaginative creation: she "seems to be on the saying of her name" (cp 339). She is summer, the world of full human satisfaction. This is a place available to the imaginative man who, like the poet of "Esthétique du Mal" and like God Himself, "establishes" it and "calls it good" (cp 324).

This is the total relationship with the visible and the invisible that Stevens sought in his poetry and the Zellers sought in their religion. The Christian religion was for

[18] "The Realistic Oriole: A Study of Wallace Stevens," *Hudson Review*, 10 (Autumn 1957), rpt. in *Critical Essays*, ed. Borroff, p. 165.

Stevens an example of a Supreme Fiction which had fully accounted for reality and fully satisfied the imagination. One of Stevens' very late poems begins, "St. Armorer's was once an immense success" (CP 529). The slight snideness in the tone should not obscure the fact that Stevens really believed the church to have been an enormously impressive and effective imaginative integration. The church, like old John Zeller, lay in his heart: he had incorporated, as his lineage and language, its forms, its words, and its symbols. They came to him almost automatically, and they formed a pattern, perhaps a paradigm, for the poetic religion he hoped to substitute for Christianity.

2

THE DEAF-MUTE CHURCH
AND THE CHAPEL OF BREATH

My direct interest is in telling the
Archbishop of Canterbury to go jump
off the end of the dock.
(LWS 351)

THE poetic religion Stevens hoped to substitute for Christianity would have nothing to do with the Archbishop of Canterbury. Stevens was, unlike T. S. Eliot, neither Anglo-Catholic, Royalist, nor Classicist, and for him the archbishop was an anachronism: not the keeper of the keys to heaven and hell, not a political force, not even a living symbol of the continuity of past and present. Things had changed utterly from the time of Thomas à Becket and the time of the Zellers, and Stevens could not return from the waste land to the Christian refuge.

The enormous pressures of twentieth-century reality come from a confusion of "events," as Stevens wrote in 1942, "that stir the emotions to violence, that engage us in what is direct and immediate and real, and . . . involve the concepts and sanctions that are the order of our lives and may involve our very lives" (NA 22). Amidst this chaos, the church had only rigidified. New realities mocked and perverted the old ceremonies, turning the once miraculous into the freakish. The church had become a "deaf-mute" (CP 357): unable to sense the new realities, unable to voice the old integrations. Like a senile

45

archbishop, it shifted with relief from the spirit to the letter, from the radiance of a life-giving fiction to the silly restrictiveness of a policeman or prude. If the archbishop could be made to jump off the dock, Stevens felt, we could substitute for the deaf-mute church a chapel of breath: a religion of poetry which might be for us what Lutheranism was for old John Zeller.

Stevens bases his critique of the church on two assumptions, both derived in part from Nietzsche. The first is that God is dead. Stevens' essay "Two or Three Ideas" considers the death of "the gods, both ancient and modern, both foreign and domestic" (op 205), and the event, as the terms of his description indicate, is as natural as it is inevitable. Their passing is, in fact, strangely anticlimactic and almost unnoticed. The gods are simply "forgotten" (op 205), "dispelled" (op 206), "denied" (cp 320); they "dissolve[d] like clouds" or, more simply, "came to nothing" (op 206). God, like Satan and Phoebus and all gods, disappeared without panache. "This vanishing of the gods," as J. Hillis Miller rightly claims, ". . . is the basis of all Stevens' thought and poetry,"[1] but it is part of a larger assumption: that "the only possible order of life is one in which all order is incessantly changing" (lws 291-292). Stevens' theory of cyclical recurrence parallels Nietzsche's idea of the *Ewiges Wiederkehr*, mentioned in "A Collect of Philosophy" (op 194) as an inherently poetic concept. Nietzsche in "Description without Place" is the type of the modern thinker: a connoisseur of seeming. As he studies the moving forms in a deep pool, his thoughts interlock with the shapes they

[1] *Poets of Reality: Six Twentieth-Century Writers* (Cambridge, Mass.: The Belknap Press of Harvard Univ. Press, 1965), p. 219.

describe so that both become "swarm-like manias / In perpetual revolution, round and round" (CP 342). Perpetual revolution, here distinguished from Lenin's particular and, for Stevens, shabby revolution, informs the universe, comprehending in its sweep the days, seasons, and years, all governments, civilizations, and eras of human belief. For each end there is a beginning: if God is dead, modern man must recognize and facilitate a new order and era of belief.

These assumptions give Stevens' critique of the church its tone and direction. In their light it is possible to accept Ralph J. Mills's assertion that "there is . . . no struggle in his verse with an older kind of orthodoxy which must be shed (unless we take 'Sunday Morning' as a partial exception); Christianity is simply observed in retrospect."[2] Stevens did struggle with nostalgia for the old Christian integrations, but he never demanded revival of a former orthodoxy. "No man," as he wrote in "Two or Three Ideas," "ever muttered a petition in his heart for the restoration of . . . unreal shapes" (OP 207). Observation in retrospect explains the frequently condescending detachment of his criticisms: the calm of a cataloguer of fossils or the scorn of a highly developed form for a vestigial one. The ability to observe in retrospect posits an evolution which has left Christianity behind.

Of Vico's three cycles—the age of the gods, the age of the heroes, and the age of man—Stevens was, as Baird points out, most interested in the second and third stages.[3]

---

[2] "Wallace Stevens: The Image of the Rock," *Accent,* 18 (Spring 1958), revised by the author and rpt. in *Critical Essays,* ed. Borroff, p. 99.

[3] *The Dome and the Rock: Structure in the Poetry of Wallace Stevens* (Baltimore: Johns Hopkins Press, 1968), p. 221.

The first stage seemed unexciting because it was almost complete. "Stevens views the progress of religions," Riddel summarizes, "as one of narrowing abstraction. It begins with the uncritical embrace of magical things and leads ultimately to their apotheosis; beyond myth, however, things are rationally distorted, ideas become rigid, and finally dogma smothers the emotional connection between man and the symbolic object."[4] This distortion and rigidity makes the full evolution of heroes and of men impossible. It is the major focus of Stevens' attack.

Since "the death of one god is the death of all" (OP 165), the death of Jove can stand for that of any other unreal shape. This has the wry and pleasant twist for Stevens of seeming safe and obvious retrospection while conspiring to overthrow the unreal shape still, though precariously, enthroned by Christianity. This tactical slyness informs some of the arguments of "Sunday Morning" and "An Ordinary Evening in New Haven."

In "Sunday Morning" the "silent shadows" (CP 67) which come between the woman and the supple, turbulent enjoyment of life symbolized by the ring of men are rigid, distorted ideas of divinity, as inappropriate as the idea of Jove. If the poet can bring her to acknowledge Jove's irrelevance, recognition of the death of the God she continues to fear will be easier. If he can demonstrate a divine evolution from Jove of "inhuman birth" (CP 67) to Christ of "our blood, commingling, virginal, / With heaven" (CP 68), she must then admit the possibility of evolution from "the thought of heaven" to a divinity that "must live within herself" (CP 67). The evolution Stevens

---

[4] "The Metaphysical Changes of Stevens' 'Esthétique du Mal,' " *Twentieth Century Literature*, 7 (July 1961), 66.

traces in Section III of "Sunday Morning" is man's progressive assumption of his full humanity. The woman is poised between the age of the gods, definitively passed, and the age of fully human heroes, tantalizing in its potentiality.

In "An Ordinary Evening in New Haven," Jove's death again represents the moment which hovers between the end of one cycle and the beginning of the next. Here, again, the death of a god is meant to suggest the death of God Himself. When Jove moved among men as a noble and profound incarnation of human belief, a god of "peremptory elevation and glory" (OP 206), the structure of ideas fitted the structure of things. He was abstract, as an intellectual and emotional construct interpreting reality, and he gave pleasure, but he could not satisfy the third criterion for a supreme fiction: he did not change. Apotheosis is possible when ideas and reality coincide; dogma is inevitable when ideas rigidify as reality changes. When Jove, once a muttering king, became a statue, ideas and things divided. The health of summer, which for Stevens marks the full union of imagination and reality, disintegrated into winter's starkness, and the imagination was helpless before reality. The old integrations stood between men and their environment and had, therefore, to be destroyed:

> It was after the neurosis of winter. It was
> In the genius of summer that they blew up
>
> The statue of Jove among the boomy clouds.
> It took all day to quieten the sky.
>
> (CP 482)

The explosion is both interior and exterior, "in space and the self" (CP 483), because the annihilation of the gods is also our annihilation: we created them, "have always shared all things with them and have always had a part of their strength and, certainly, all of their knowledge" (OP 207). The quiet after the explosion defines the vacancy between one supreme fiction and another:

There was a clearing, a readiness for first bells,
An opening for outpouring, the hand was raised:
There was a willingness not yet composed,

A knowing that something certain had been proposed,
Which, without the statue, would be new,
An escape from repetition, a happening.
(CP 483)

The goal of Stevens' critique of the deaf-mute church is this escape from repetition into the moment of vibrant potentiality, the clearing and the readiness which, Stevens feels, should be ours, now and here.

In death, the Judeo-Christian God is already a statue, as fixed and as oblivious to the changing world as Stevens' other pompous, forgotten stone statesmen. Stevens' critique of Christianity is his attempt to blow up that statue. Perhaps because he found Christian formulations obviously irrelevant, perhaps because he doubted his competence in theological argument,[5] perhaps because he considered the Christian creed more an outmoded aesthetic projection than a serious object of belief, Stevens rarely

[5] Mills calls attention to some of Stevens' "misconceptions of traditional Christianity" in "Wallace Stevens: The Image of the Rock," *Critical Essays*, ed. Borroff, p. 99.

seemed to notice Christian dogma in itself. His usual method was to juxtapose the rigidified belief to the fluid forces of reality: natural, personal, social, or political. In a time of possible expansion and evolution, Stevens argued, the church is a narrowing, negative, exclusive influence. His three major criticisms, which it will be useful to explore in some detail, are that it rejects life, it rejects doubt, and it rejects the self which alone, for Stevens, creates a "synthesis on which to rely" (LWS 403).

Life in Stevens' formulations is the male principle: the booted, belted, arrogant force usually symbolized by the sun. The sun is "that brave man" who "comes up / From below and walks without meditation" (CP 138). It is the day flashing its strength—"the youth, the vital son, the heroic power" (CP 375). Flauntingly fertile, it rises as "bull fire" (CP 198), and in its light we see "everything bulging and blazing and big in itself" (CP 205). The sun is, in sum, "male reality" (OP 99), and it shines "on whatever the earth happens to be" (OP 130). It does not, however, shine on high-toned old Christian women. The church for Stevens is a widow, and not because, as in patristic exegesis, it is married to Christ who has gone to heaven. It is a widow because it is separated from life itself. The ordinary women, the high-toned old Christian woman, the lady dying of diabetes in "A Thought Revolved," and Canon Aspirin's sister in "Notes toward a Supreme Fiction" share the qualities Stevens attributes to the church and its sycophants: dreary asceticism, mechanical ritualism, Puritanical primness, and an attenuated ghostliness which makes them seem to drift rather than stride, to exist rather than live.

"The Ordinary Women" is, Riddel comments, "an elegant sport with religious imagery, turning a ritual of

asceticism into a ritual of epicureanism."[6] The arch irony
of the poem, however, is in its symmetry; for these
women there is little difference between asceticism and
epicureanism. Absolute Christianity, Stevens seems to say,
corrupts absolutely, so that when the women seek an
opposite they are doomed to find a parallel. The poem
contrasts the ordinary house which the women flee with
the Palace of Art which they enter. Each point of comparison emphasizes divorce from life. "Then," the poem
begins, as if continuing an old and fitful story, "from
their poverty they rose" (CP 10). Poverty is a Christian
virtue because it enforces a healthy separation from the
physical in preparation for the spirituality of the kingdom
of heaven. For Stevens, it is a vice. "The greatest poverty," as "Esthétique du Mal" defines it, "is not to live /
In a physical world" (CP 325); this, as the line division
hints, is not to live at all. The poverty the women believe
they can turn from—"their want" (CP 10), their emptiness, their spiritual dryness—reappears in the palace's
"gaunt guitarists" (CP 11). "Then," the last stanza begins,
"from their poverty they rose" (CP 12).

The qualities which particularize the vapidness of both
worlds form a paradigm of poverty for Stevens: dryness,
coldness, disease, monotony, and flitting ghostliness. Like
the paralyzing "neurosis of winter" in "An Ordinary
Evening," they grip both earth and heaven. The ordinary
women's "dry catarrhs" (CP 10) complement the aridness
of the palace's "dry guitars" (CP 12), so that the guitarists' rumbling and mumbling song resounds like tubercular
coughing. The women's flight from poverty, catarrhs,
and monotony is a blind search for salvation, for "the
hullaballoo of health and have" (CP 292):

[6] *Clairvoyant Eye*, p. 64.

This halloo, halloo, halloo heard over the cries

Of those for whom a square room is a fire,
Of those whom the statues torture and keep down.

This health is holy, this descant of a self,
This barbarous chanting of what is strong, this blare.

(CP 191)

Salvation for Stevens is accomplished in elemental merging with the strength and blare of earth; for the women,
it retains its Christian meaning of liberation from the phe-
nomenal world and final union with ultimate reality. The
lacquered, nocturnal palace is a refined denial of the
physical, but once there the women, kept down by Christian forms, can merge with nothing: they "study / The
canting curlicues // Of heaven and of the heavenly
script," they "read of marriage-bed" (CP 11). They are
ghosts damned by their own illusory Christian hopes to
roam in limbo, to flit between the heaven they cannot
make real and the earth they cannot escape.

The vacillation between asceticism and epicureanism in
"The Ordinary Women" forms a pseudo-debate; the
conflict is interior and the opposing terms ultimately
merge. "A High-Toned Old Christian Woman" (CP 59),
on the other hand, is part of a true debate. The high-
toned woman, advocate of "the moral law," and the high-
handed poet, advocate of "bawdiness," match fictions,
and the poet's argument is again that Christianity rejects
the "jovial hullabaloo" of life. The debater compares
point for point the widow's existence and the reveler's
life, the ascetic and the epicurean, the Christian and the
poetic: for the Christian nave there is a pagan peri-

style, for hankering citherns squiggling saxophones, for "haunted heaven" a "masque / Beyond the planets," for conscience's constrictions the fling of indulgence. At every point, poetry is "supreme" or, with sly variations on the root meaning of "supreme," highest. In a reversal of Christian doctrine, on which the poet sophistically assumes he and his opponent "agree in principle," heaven did not delegate authority to the church: the moral law created the church and the church in turn built a heaven haunted by moral phantoms. Poetry projects a higher masque, one which reaches into "the planetary scene" to reside "among the spheres." If tonal range is at issue, squiggling saxophones outdo windy citherns. And, finally, the Christian woman's high tone is mere sanctimoniousness, but the revelers' music is an elevation to "the sublime." The revelers are not gaunt like the guitarists but "well-stuffed," rowdy, and proud. They have rejected the epitaphs of the moral law and wink with the carnival barker's joy in life, in fact "wink most when widows wince."

"A High-Toned Old Christian Woman" is, as Riddel notes, "not so much a denunciation of old Christian women as a defense of poetry."[7] When Stevens can resist comparing poetry and Christianity, the result is, like Section 1 of "A Thought Revolved," more savage than sportive. The contest between Mrs. Grundy and the life principle is one-sided, but "the struggle of the idea of god / And the idea of man" (CP 185) is not. The thought revolved in this poem is the evolution of an "earthly leader" (CP 185), a "man / Of men whose heaven is in themselves" (CP 186). The idea of God, even in its de-

---

[7] *Clairvoyant Eye*, p. 73.

generation a tenacious and formidable obstacle to the
advent of this leader, is represented here by "the mechanical optimist" (CP 184). The optimist has, like the
snow man, neither life nor self. He clings to the old
order: the advent of Christ announced, as if to emphasize
its distant unreality, over the radio. Contemporary religion is, for Stevens, a thought which revolves not progressively, like Nietzsche's meditation by the pool, but
blandly and automatically like the "priestly gramophones" (CP 141) of "Winter Bells." The assurances of
"the night before Christmas and all the carols" (CP 185)
have become as stale as they are cheerful: as once the
promise was birth, now the prospect, for the optimist
who ignores things as they are, is slow death.

The mechanical optimist is another of Stevens' ghostly
and fitful widows: "a lady dying of diabetes" (CP 184).
The word "diabetes" doubly emphasizes "die," but, in
Stevens' meticulousness, it was probably chosen as much
for its symptoms as for its sounds. The disease is his diag-
nosis of contemporary religion. One symptom of diabetes
is excessive sugar in the blood and urine—an objective
correlative for the nostalgia, sentimentality, and self-pity
which, in Stevens' view, saturates the church. The lady
envisions a death as comfortable and picturesque as the
radio's version of Christ's birth:

> It seemed serener just to die,
> To float off in the floweriest barge,
>
> Accompanied by the exegesis
> Of familiar things in a cheerful voice.
>   (CP 184-185)

Popular exegesis, in its emphasis on the flowery and the cheerful, apparently includes among its scriptural texts Tennyson's "The Lady of Shalott." Excessive sugar in diabetes, like excessive sentimentality in belief, occasions thirst and hunger. In an age when "heaven collects its bleating lambs" (CP 184) over the radio, the sheep are not fed. They hunger for connection with reality: "Feed my lambs," Stevens demanded in the "Adagia," "(on the bread of living)" (OP 178). Mechanical and optimistic myths offer death rather than life. The idea of God is one of these myths.

That the widow in Stevens' poetry is the church and its debilitated believers is hinted in "The Ordinary Women," "A High-Toned Old Christian Woman," and "A Thought Revolved," but it is most strongly suggested in the portrait, from "Notes toward a Supreme Fiction," of Canon Aspirin's sister. "Probably," Baird notes, "she is Ecclesia."[8] Epitomizing the traits of the other women, she is drab, poor, rigid, and ascetic. She denies life so thoroughly that even her ecstasy is "sensible" (CP 401). Her two daughters, "one / Of four, and one of seven" (CP 402), are, like Crispin's daughters, the projections of imagination. Also like Crispin's daughters, they are vague enough to madden the critic, but their ages, matching two of the most prevalent sacred numbers, hint that they might be equivalent to such things as the four evangelists and the seven sacred virtues. "Appropriate to / Their poverty," they are pale in her "rigid statement of them." They are like drab sermons ornamented only by the clichés of religious wisdom: "Sunday pearls, her widow's gayety" (CP 402). Her rigidity, in defiance of life's profusion, excludes the complex and mysterious from her

---

[8] *The Dome and the Rock*, p. 26.

own formulations as from her daughters' consciousness. She demands "only the unmuddled self of sleep, for them" and holds them "closelier to her by rejecting dreams" (CP 402). Sleep in Christian exegesis is sometimes valuable because, like poverty, it removes us from the corrupt physical world, but for Stevens sleep is usually criminal neglect of life:

> Of the two dreams, night and day,
> What lover, what dreamer, would choose
> The one obscured by sleep?
> (CP 89)

Sleep is also valuable to the Christian because it facilitates communion with the spiritual through dream, but the widow's rejection of dream-experience, experience like Will's in *Piers Plowman* or Adam's in *Paradise Lost*, makes her children's sleep mere death-in-life. Denying both the physical and the spiritual, the widow has, Stevens comments with a dryness he often reserves for the church, "never explored anything at all and shrinks from doing so" (LWS 445).

Just as the man of men in "A Thought Revolved" balances the lady dying of diabetes, so Canon Aspirin, the poet as his own priest and the maker of his own belief, balances his sister. He, in the true ecstasy or bodilessness of soaring dream, chooses affirmation over negation, life over death:

> He chose to include the things
> That in each other are included, the whole,
> The complicate, the amassing harmony.
> (CP 403)

If the widow's daughters are to be saved and the formulations of the church revitalized, it will not be through sanctimonious denial but through the liberating imagination the Canon brings as he descends to the children's bed. The Canon is his sister's obverse—neither rigid, poor, nor ascetic. In choosing life, he must choose not her "barest phrase" but his own "fugue / Of praise" (CP 402).

The church's barest phrase rejects life on its most vital physical level. It also rejects doubt, the necessary condition for a life of the mind. As denial of the physical makes Stevens' widows thin and sickly, so rejection of doubt makes his erudite doctors stolid and ridiculous. "The Doctor of Geneva" and "The Blue Buildings in the Summer Air" draw a devastating portrait of the Puritan mind: in each, the systematic theologian confronts chaos, refuses to alter his tidy but irrelevant structure of ideas, and consequently suffers, like the pompous man who slips on a banana peel, a cruel but laughable pratfall.

Stevens fully enjoys his sport with the stiff-necked, self-righteous Doctor of Geneva (CP 24). The classically comic spectacle of a man competent in one environment blundering outrageously in another serves Stevens well as he translates the limited "lacustrine man" to the Pacific shore, "the wild, the ruinous waste." Crispin before the sea found his "mythology of self, / Blotched out beyond unblotching" (CP 28), but if he fumbles pitifully, he yet accepts doubt and changes. The Calvinist cannot. Stamping the sand, adjusting his stovepipe hat and his shawl, the Doctor thwarts doubt with pride, fooling himself but not us:

He did not quail. A man so used to plumb
The multifarious heavens felt no awe
Before these visible, voluble delugings.

The man who plumbs the heavens with Latinate elo-
quence ignores the blunt reality of his "simmering mind /
Spinning and hissing" on the verge of explosion. A second
comic device—the deflation of a pretentious mind by its
insistent body—provides this explosion. If, in theological exegesis, the head is the city of God, perhaps the
nose is its steeple. The Doctor, quailing in the sea air,
sneezes:

> the steeples of his city clanked and sprang
> In an unburgherly apocalypse.
> The doctor used his handkerchief and sighed.

He is about to catch an ordinary dry catarrh.

The mouse of "The Blue Buildings in the Summer
Air" is to Cotton Mather, another militant Puritan, as the
sea to the Doctor of Geneva. It is all that evades a rigid,
intellectualized scheme of ideas, a scheme such as Mather's
attempt in *Magnalia Christi Americana* to demonstrate
the working of God's will in the early history of Massa-
chusetts. The mouse embodies time and change and
works to reduce everything to chaos: its "eminent thun-
der" is "the grinding in the arches of the church, /
The plaster dropping, even dripping, down" (CP 217).
It is, as Daniel Fuchs explains, "the power behind the
throne, more god than God, the last omnipotence";[9] its
law is change in the structure of things, and this neces-

---

[9] *The Comic Spirit of Wallace Stevens*, p. 77.

sitates doubt in the structure of ideas. To maintain
certitude, Mather must ignore the mouse:

> There was always the doubt,
> That made him preach the louder, long for a church
> In which his voice would roll its cadences,
> After the sermon, to quiet that mouse in the wall.
>
> (CP 216)

The suppression of doubt fortifies order, but order is an
ambiguous virtue. Order at the expense of things as they
are is, like the sleep of Canon Aspirin's nieces, death-in-
life.

Stevens judges Mather, with a wink, by the Puritan
ethic, and the joke is that ultimately "the books / He
read, all day, all night and all the nights, / Had got him
nowhere" (CP 216). Thinking heaven is there when it
is here, Mather ends up neither here nor there:

> Look down now, Cotton Mather, from the blank.
> Was heaven where you thought? It must be there.
> It must be where you think it is, in the light
> On bed-clothes, in an apple on a plate.
>
> (CP 217)

Heaven, Mather reasoned, must be where the necessities
of his system deduced it to be. It is, in fact, where the
system is not: in time, change, and the cycle of fruition
and decay. Doubt is the recognition of change. By rejecting doubt, ironically and sadly, religion rejects both
heaven and earth.

The rejection of doubt is the choice of systematic
form over spontaneous intuition, exterior over interior,

the mighty fortress of the church over "one's own fortitude of spirit," the strength which is, for Stevens, "the
only 'fester Burg' " (LWS 403). In rejecting life and
doubt, the church rejects the self. Selflessness, like poverty and the abstraction of sleep, is a Christian virtue,
for the self is obstinate in its attachment to the physical
world. For Eliot, as for the Christian fathers, it is an
obstacle in "the time of tension between dying and
birth,"[10] between death to this world and birth into the
kingdom of God. The agony of "Ash Wednesday" is
the struggle to destroy the insistent self and thereby to
attain a selflessness in which we know "our peace in His
will."[11] This is also the agony of Thomas à Becket's
fourth and most unexpected temptation: the continua-
tion of the self in eternity through the obliteration of
the self in time, enduring glory through martyrdom. His
soul's sickness defines itself as the inability to destroy his
will, the vitality of the self. For Stevens, this is nonsense,
since life is and can only be the action of the will in
time. We live in

> The rich earth, of its own self made rich,
> Fertile of its own leaves and days and wars,
> Of its brown wheat rapturous in the wind,
> The nature of its women in the air.
>
> (CP 491)

These, the things the penitent of "Ash Wednesday"
would transcend, are our glory. Life, doubt, change, and
spontaneity form for Stevens the "descant of a self"

[10] *The Complete Poems and Plays: 1909-1950* (New York:
Harcourt, Brace & World, 1952), p. 66.
[11] *Complete Poems and Plays*, p. 67.

(CP 191), of the spirit which gives life. The church is the literalist which kills: it "stands for little more than propriety" (LWS 348) and it exalts certitude, rigidity, and formalization. Men retreat into it when the self no longer suffices, and, once inside, the self, become one with an unchanging structure of ideas and regulations, vanishes. A series of poems from *Ideas of Order*, which might take as epigraph "the letter killeth, but the spirit giveth life" (II Corinthians 3.6), contrasts the church's paralysis with the self's vitality.

"Waving Adieu, Adieu, Adieu" and "Anglais Mort à Florence" balance these two ideas of order—the idea of God and the idea of man, or, as "The Man with the Blue Guitar" defines them, "that gold self aloft" and "a substitute for all the gods: / This self" (CP 176)—to show that as the one diminishes the other increases. To wave adieu, or, the same thing, to wave *à dieu*, is to understand that we live "in a world without heaven to follow" (CP 127). "We are," Stevens explains, "physical beings in a physical world" (LWS 348). This exacts as severe a discipline as religion itself, and "one likes to practice the thing. They practice, / Enough, for heaven" (CP 128). Whereas practicing for heaven is constraint, however, practicing for earth is liberation. It is "waving and . . . / Crying and shouting" (CP 127); it is being so fully we cannot be taught not to care; it is

> To be one's singular self, to despise
> The being that yielded so little, acquired
> So little, too little to care, to turn
> To the ever-jubilant weather.
> (CP 127-128)

In bidding farewell to God, the spirit grows strong enough to stand alone. "Just to be there and just to behold" (CP 127) suffices. The poignancy of "Anglais Mort à Florence" is that for the Englishman, as for other of Stevens' phantoms, "to be is not enough / To be" (CP 320):

> But he remembered the time when he stood alone,
> When to be and delight to be seemed to be one,
> Before the colors deepened and grew small.
>
> (CP 149)

The movement of this poem reverses that of "Waving Adieu": as rejecting religion brought acceptance of life, so rejecting life brings dependence upon religion. "Most people stand by the aid of philosophy, religion and one thing or another," Stevens commented, "but a strong spirit (Anglais, etc.) stands by its own strength. Even such a spirit is subject to degeneration" (LWS 348). Two movements mark this degeneration: a turning away from the jubilant weather and a turning toward religion. In the collapse of the Englishman's spirit, "a little less returned for him each spring" (CP 148); the colors faded; the moon "had grown cadaverous" (CP 149). As joy failed, he practiced for heaven by denying instinct and, like the Doctor of Geneva and Cotton Mather, exalting reason. In his final diminishment, and in one of Stevens' more devastating equations, "he stood at last by God's help and the police" (CP 149).

This sense of diminishment informs another group of poems from *Ideas of Order*: "A Fading of the Sun," "Gray Stones and Gray Pigeons," and "Winter Bells."

The thesis of these three poems against the church is that
the death of religious forms both stems from and leads
to the death of the spirit. For Stevens, the defining
characteristic of the self is its "blessed rage for order"
(CP 130), the instinct to confront and conquer chaos by
fashioning "one's own synthesis on which to rely" out
of "one's own fortitude of spirit." The diminished self,
submitting helplessly to chaos, turns with relief to the
absence of life: fading light, neutral color, the stark
suspension of winter. The Jew of "Winter Bells" aban-
dons himself to religious forms, the automatism of
"priestly gramophones" and "regulations of his spirit,"
to soothe his one remaining sign of life: "his rage against
chaos" (CP 141). He looks outward for the solace which,
"A Fading of the Sun" explains, comes only from within.
Joy, for the lost and confused,

> lies, themselves within themselves,
> If they will look
> Within themselves
> And cry and cry for help.
>   (CP 139)

It is not the exterior structure of the church but the
self's interior fortitude which gives order, which stands
"within as pillars of the sun, / Supports of night" (CP
139).

"Gray Stones and Gray Pigeons" accomplishes Stevens' wish to have the archbishop jump off the end of the
dock. On the surface, this is a simple desire for the disappearance of an anachronism, but, given Stevens' habit
of thought, it is possible that the wish is not wholly
flippant and destructive. To jump off the dock is to

leave the safety of a stable system and to immerse one-self, for Stevens as for Conrad, in the destructive element. The archbishop of this poem has jumped from fixity to flux, from blankness to color, from paralysis to vitality. He represents the living spirit which has deserted the church. "Everything," Stevens explains, "depends on its sanction; and when its sanction is lost that is the end of it" (LWS 347). Religious forms have, like Jove and Satan, come to a quiet yet definite end: "The archbishop is away. The church is gray" (CP 140). The self, once the vital soul of the church, now is "globed in today and tomorrow"; the archbishop, once the minister of eternal, ethereal fire, now "walks / Among fireflies" (CP 140), in the midst of flickering, ephemeral, spontaneous and unsponsored physical vitality.

Stevens rarely wrote good poetry out of negation. The blankness of poems like "Winter Bells" and "Anglais Mort à Florence" comes not from any wavering in Stevens' criticisms but from the stark vision of the vacuum between the negation of one supreme fiction and the affirmation of another. "For the sensitive poet, conscious of negations," Stevens wrote in "The Noble Rider and the Sound of Words," "nothing is more difficult than the affirmations of nobility and yet there is nothing that he requires of himself more persistently, since in them and in their kind, alone, are to be found those sanctions that are the reasons for his being and for that occasional ecstasy, or ecstatic freedom of the mind, which is his special privilege" (NA 35). The most remarkable thing about the annihilation of the statue of Jove is not the explosion itself but the quieting of the sky afterwards, the emptiness that must be refilled (CP 482). In the same way, Satan's disappearance is neither

threatening nor astonishing, but the cold vacancy it
creates is both (CP 320). Negation is easy, but suspension of belief is for Stevens impossible. "If one no longer
believes in God (as truth)," Stevens wrote Hi Simons in
1940, "it is not possible merely to disbelieve; it becomes
necessary to believe in something else" (LWS 370).

The something else which replaced the deaf-mute
church was the chapel of breath. Though the chapel
of breath appears late in Stevens' work, it is a summation
of values present from the beginning. A culmination of
Stevens' search for a substitute for Christianity, it is both
evolution and revolution from the deaf-mute church.
There is a massive difference between the two, but they
are alike as affirmations of nobility, sanctions for being,
causes of ecstasy, and reasons for freedom. They are
supreme fictions, one adequate in the past, one, like the
archbishop, globed in today and tomorrow. The qualities of the chapel of breath are suggested by the fireflies
which balance the gray church and its gray pigeons that
cannot fly. The chapel of breath is ephemeral and radiant, a vital, physical continuum which, like the burning
star of "Martial Cadenza," is life itself:

>   the ever-living and being,
>   The ever-breathing and moving, the constant fire,
>
> IV
>
> The present close, the present realized,
> Not the symbol but that for which the symbol stands.
>
> (CP 238)

Only in evolving beyond Christianity can we liberate
the increasingly human self; only in seeing St. Armorer's

Church "from the outside" can we realize the chapel of breath.

Baird dates "St. Armorer's Church from the Outside" in the last year of Stevens' life.[12] It summarizes his critique of the church and exemplifies his transvaluation of Christian symbols into the living emblems of a new creed. Like Yeats's "The Circus Animals' Desertion" and Stevens' own "As You Leave the Room," the poem draws on an entire poetic canon for its resonance and to explicate it is to touch on many of the major themes. "St. Armorer's," it begins, "was once an immense success" (CP 529), but now the church, like the saint, is unbesought and unimportant. Like armor, it has lost its usefulness, declining from a necessity into a clanking superfluity. Its defects now were its virtues then, for the very massiveness of its protective covering has made it a prison. St. Armorer's, like a stout suit of metal, "fixed one for good" (CP 529); in the chapel of breath, on the other hand, one "walks and does as he lives and likes" (CP 530). Man-made as a thorough defense against death, the church, like armor, was pathetically ineffectual against the natural changes of mortality. "What is left" of St. Armorer's is musty decay: "the foreign smell of plaster, / The closed-in smell of hay" (CP 529). The forces symbolized by the mouse in "Blue Buildings," forces manifested in "the plaster dropping, even dripping, down" (CP 217), and those suggested in "Credences of Summer" by the hay in Oley, "baked through long days . . . piled in mows" (CP 374), have made the church the victim of its own rigidity. It is claustrophobic and alien. It has, Stevens summarizes,

---

[12] *The Dome and the Rock*, p. 3.

nothing of this present,
This *vif*, this dizzle-dazzle of being new
And of becoming, for which the chapel spreads out
Its arches in its vivid element.

(CP 530)

The vivid element in which the chapel exists is both being and becoming, the presence of space and the continuing presentness of time.

The chapel is "like a new account of everything old"
(CP 529), but its newness incorporates an older paradigm: the church's words, forms, and symbols. It is "a
sacred syllable rising from sacked speech" (CP 530), the
speech of the church which came to Stevens as his lineage and language. Before shaping the tentative beginnings
of a new religion, however, the speech had to be cleansed
of cliché. In a sense what Stevens does here is what in
"Lions in Sweden" he urges Swenson to do: if the fault
is with the sovereign images, "send them back / . . .
whence they came. / The vegetation still abounds with
forms" (CP 125). The symbols of Christianity in St. Armorer's church have receded to their origin, a source
from which they can rise once more as sacred syllables.
Christ's Tree, the cross, has become "a sumac grow[ing]
/ On the altar" (CP 529). The Lord "that was the true
Light, which lighteth every man" (John 1.9) has de-
ferred to the sun, the natural light toward which the
sumac stretches. The Word in its collapse has reverted
to uncontained sound, "reverberations [which] leak and
lack among holes" (CP 529). Stevens' effort was to create out of these ruins new affirmations, to place amid the
"dead blaze" and "cindery noes" of Christianity "an
ember yes" (CP 529).

The imagination is the power which allows this new account and affirmation. It is the word and also, for Stevens, the light. Imagination, as "The Figure of the Youth as Virile Poet" defines it, is a sun to supersede both Son and Father:

Like light, it adds nothing, except itself. What light requires a day to do, and by day I mean a kind of Biblical revolution of time, the imagination does in the twinkling of an eye. It colors, increases, brings to a beginning and end, invents languages, crushes men and, for that matter, gods in its hands, it says to women more than it is possible to say, it rescues all of us from what we have called absolute fact and while it does these things, and more, it makes sure that

> . . . *la mandoline jase,*
> *Parmi les frissons de brise.*
> (NA 61-62)

Inevitably it penetrates the armor of the church, as "a new-colored sun, say, that will soon change forms / And spread hallucinations on every leaf" (CP 529). The hallucinations are, like our old hallucinations, fictions, but with this difference: they do not fix us but allow us to be and to become.

By the creed of St. Armorer's, to enter true or ever-lasting life men had first "to lie / In its church-yard," to be translated to the "geranium-colored day" (CP 529) of heaven. For Stevens, to believe this is to be buried; to reject it is to rise into being or, in an image of birth and resurrection, to be "the first car out of a tunnel en voy-age // Into lands of ruddy-ruby fruits" (CP 530). The chapel of breath "rises from Terre Ensevelie" (CP 529), from what Arnold called our "buried life . . . the mystery of this heart which beats / So wild, so deep in us."[13] It rises from the self that Christianity stifles, from the "dreamers buried in our sleep" (CP 39), from our own fortitude of spirit and rage for order. Whereas in Christianity, for Stevens, exterior order, or regulations of the spirit imposed from without, creates an interior blank in which we are deprived even of our rage against chaos, the chapel creates out of exterior chaos an interior order: "a civilization formed from the outward blank" (CP 529). A civilization rising from within is to one imposed from without as skin is to armor. Where one evolves naturally, the other confines artificially. Where one allows expansion in "an air of freshness, clearness, greenness, blue-ness" (CP 530), the other's "closed-in smell" (CP 529) is smothering.

The idea of a chapel of breath to counter the stony bulwarks of the Christian church evolved gradually in Stevens' poetry. If the builders of the Christian churches created out of faith for the glory of God, Stevens wrote out of imagination for the glory of poetry. Architecture, as the creation of visible order from fragments of reality, became one of his major figures for the act of design or discipline of shaping. The building, like the poem, is imagination come to form momentarily to express the dream, and thus the poet, or major man, or "ultimate politician," is also for Stevens the ultimate architect:

[13] "The Buried Life," in *Poetry and Criticism of Matthew Arnold*, ed. Culler, p. 114.

He is the final builder of the total building,
The final dreamer of the total dream,
Or will be. Building and dream are one.

(CP 335)

He is a politician because he contends with the evolution of society: he meditates the past, the dilapidated building which stands, here as elsewhere in Stevens' work, for an interrupted dream (CP 336), and the future, the total building and the total dream. He is a poet because he is the man who deals most with imagination (dream) and reality (building). As a poet-politician, he labors to make his fictions fact, to accomplish his dream in a building or to incarnate his structure of ideas in a structure of things. Buildings are "men turning into things" (CP 470), and they ruthlessly reveal the truth of the builders' beliefs. For this reason, as a note from "Adagia" explains, "There is no difference between god and his temple" (OP 164). New gods necessitate new temples, and, conversely, the building of new temples is the creation of new gods.

As early as 1918, in the poem "Architecture," Stevens worked on a blueprint for a temple of "the lusty and the plenteous" (OP 18). The poem, although slight, is significant in its intentions and in its failure. Like Matisse at Vence, Stevens would design his church in its entirety: exterior, interior, windows, frescoes, vestments, even the "heavenly dithyramb" (OP 16) and "speech . . . / In that splay of marble" (OP 17). The thoroughness with which he wanted to imitate the church, while banishing its "holy or sublime ado" (OP 18), matches the completeness of his bewilderment at how to do it. Sections II and

III consist entirely of questions which Sections IV and V answer with the vague projection of a "building of light" (OP 17) buttressed by "coral air / And purple timbers" (OP 18).

The building of light embodies the air and illumination which St. Armorer's lacks, but as a new temple it is unsatisfactory both in its aim and in its construction. As a "chastel de chasteté" (OP 16), its aim is to deify purity. The word *chastel* is perhaps intended to recall the Provençal word *castel* (i.e., *château*) and to combine the sounds of *chasteté* and *chapelle*, but the purity the name stresses is problematic. It is not freedom from the physical, from harshness, or from taint, nor does it seem abstraction, since the lusty are its devotees. It is not deprivation, for the plenteous worship there. Without concentrated strength, the purity it exalts seems finally only a sort of frivolity and preciousness that makes the Christian church seem indeed a mighty fortress. In its construction, the new temple's flimsiness had the advantage of flexibility: it was to be as expansive as its evolving faith, a structure of things which might change with the structure of ideas. The development of the idea, however, stops abruptly in the confusing suggestion that we "never cease to deploy" the building of light but "pass the whole of life earing the clink of the / Chisels of the stone-cutters cutting the stones" (OP 16). Stevens never reprinted the poem, but he also never ceased to attempt to perfect its ideas.

In "Botanist on Alp (No. 2)" and "Evening without Angels" from *Ideas of Order* and "The Blue Buildings in the Summer Air" from *Parts of a World*, Stevens found an easier solution. For the confining domes of Christian architecture, he would substitute "the sparkling Byzantine" (CP 217) of the sky. This has several virtues: it makes the earth itself a temple, it implies constant fluctuation, and it hints the vastness Stevens claimed for the imagination's domain, since the deity enthroned in the "blue building" (CP 216), in "the bays of heaven, brighted, blued" (CP 136), is, of course, the imagination. But the dome of the sky is also unsatisfactory as a substitute for the church. To abstract imagination from the mind and enthrone it in the sky differs little from what Stevens scorned in conventional religion: "For convenience, and in view of the simplicity of the large mass of people, we give our good qualities to God, or to various gods, but they come from ourselves" (LWS 295). To project our good qualities upwards makes the sky, as Christianity did, a "dividing and indifferent blue," not, as Stevens prophesied for the new faith, "a part of labor and a part of pain" (CP 68). The sky has nothing of ourselves: we are not its architect, we cannot reside there. For Stevens, who always relished the fascination of what is difficult, the metaphor of the sky as dome is finally boring, neither a challenge nor a revelation.

Owl's Clover, written between *Ideas of Order* and *Parts of a World*, formulates a third plan for Stevens' personal church. This, "the spirit's episcopate, hallowed and high" (OP 53), combines elements of the two previous sketches. The domain of the spirit is in the sky, but more modestly than "Botanist" and "Blue Buildings" imply. The picture is somewhat confusing, but the episcopate seems to be part of a collection of domes not unlike the kremlin "Architecture" mentions. Baird sees it as "an earthly paradise of domes, each man the possessor of his middle dome among the structures of other men."[14]

[14] *The Dome and the Rock*, p. 11.

Above the domes spreads the sky: "an upper dome"
which is "stippled / By waverings of stars." Below each
middle dome is a church: "the temple of the altar where
each man / Beheld the truth and knew it to be true."
The Byzantine dome topping a Gothic structure of "long
cloud-cloister-porches" (OP 54) is a plan which combines the celestial loftiness of "Blue Buildings" with the
churchly structure of the building of light, but what it
gains in intricacy it loses in clarity and immediacy.

Like the chastel de chasteté, the spirit's episcopate is
airy and radiant, but Stevens attempts to give it a more
definite conceptual substance. It consists of light, and
within it each man's solitude is

Like a solitude of the sun, in which the mind
Acquired transparence and beheld itself
And beheld the source from which transparence came.

(OP 54)

Stevens uses the word "transparence," to become a major symbolic concept in the later poetry, for the first
time in *Owl's Clover*. Transparence is a state of mind in
which, all invented theories banished, we see into the
life of things: inward to the mind, outward to the source
of the mind's images. The transparence of the spirit's
episcopate, however, like the purity of the chastel, is
tentative and undeveloped. It conveys more the elfin
charm of the building of light than the symbolic radiance implied by transparence in later poems. The spirit's
episcopate is, in the end, no more satisfying a substitute
for the church than the building of light or dome of the
sky. It cannot change; it is not natural; it does not seem
part of the self. As a structure, it is as fanciful and fussy

as a Walt Disney castle. As a concept, it must strain to embody Stevens' ideas.

The chapel of breath is the culmination of the search begun in "Architecture." It is, Stevens explains in "St. Armorer's," "Matisse at Vence and a great deal more than that" (CP 529). In his vitality, love of color and of intricate pattern, Stevens has often been compared to Matisse.[15] Both men in old age strove to mate their earthy joyousness with spiritual celebration. The Chapel of the Rosary of the Dominican Nuns of Vence was completed in the eighty-second year of Matisse's life. "This chapel is for me," he wrote, "the conclusive achievement of a whole life of labour and the flowering of a huge, sincere, and difficult striving. . . . I regard it, despite all its imperfections, as my masterpiece . . . as an effort which is the culmination of a whole life dedicated to the search for truth."[16] Stevens' chapel of breath is, in the same way, a conclusive achievement and a flowering, for it embodies the values of a life dedicated to the search for a substitute for religion. The chapel is, in the biblical tones of "St. Armorer's," "an appearance made / For a sign of meaning in the meaningless" (CP 529); it goes beyond Catholicism, which had for Stevens become part of the meaningless, into the harder architecture of a new faith. In this way, it means, humbly and tentatively, "a great deal more" than the chapel at Vence.

[15] See, for instance, Miller, *Poets of Reality*, p. 237; Baird, *The Dome and the Rock*, p. 155; and Robert Buttel, *Wallace Stevens: The Making of Harmonium* (Princeton: Princeton Univ. Press, 1967), pp. 158-159.

[16] The chapel pamphlet guide published by the Congregation of the Dominican Nuns of Monteils Aveyron, quoted by Baird, *The Dome and the Rock*, p. 311.

The use of breath as a symbol seems in Stevens' later poetry so simple and natural as to be almost inevitable, yet it came to him after difficult striving. For each physical implication, there are spiritual resonances which he had attempted to capture through various, often labored, symbolic constructs. In the chapel of breath, formed of the arches of air we inhale and exhale, they come together as one to defy the deaf-mute church and to define a religion which accepts life, doubt, and the self.

The chapel of breath is a radical return to the source of sovereign symbols, a return from the artificial to the natural, from the created object to the creating force. It is also a return to Stevens' youthful Emersonianism, for it makes of a physical fact a divine force or "sacred syllable." Even the word "breath" is a return to a root, for if, as Emerson argued in "Nature," "every word which is used to express a moral or intellectual fact, if traced to its root, is found to be borrowed from some material appearance,"[17] Stevens may have been tracing to its source an example Emerson himself used: the radical meaning of the Latin *spiritus* is wind or breath, and the chapel of breath is the chapel of the spirit. Unlike the building of light, the sky as dome, or the spirit's episcopate, it rises out of the self and sustains the self.

The action of breathing is a mutually sustaining and mutually modifying interchange of self and environment, invisible and visible, imagination and reality. It figures the process Stevens takes to be the essence of life: the intercourse of the self and the not-self. We inhale what is not ourselves, make it ours by merging with it, and

[17] *Selections from Ralph Waldo Emerson*, ed. Stephen E. Whicher (Cambridge, Mass.: Riverside Press, 1957), p. 31.

exhale it back into things as they are. Imagination changes reality and reality modifies imagination in a process Stevens explains through a rather labored metaphor from "The Man with the Blue Guitar." The poet's aim is

> That I may reduce the monster to
> Myself, and then may be myself
>
> In face of the monster, be more than part
> Of it.
>
> (CP 175)

The monster is, of course, things as they are, "what one faces" (LWS 360). We absorb it, as we absorb air, by reducing it to ourselves or making it ours; then we release it in order to confront it again as an equal. In absorption, the poet, or imagination, and the monster, or reality, become "two together as one" (CP 175); in release, whatever self the monster has is the self the poet gives it, and the self of the poet bears the monster as "its intelligence" (CP 175).

"Two Illustrations That the World Is What You Make of It," a late poem, recasts this idea in a more natural metaphor: the process of breathing. The wind, "large and loud and high and strong," was at first to the thinking man as the sea to the singer at Key West or to the Doctor of Geneva—"not his thought, nor anyone's"—yet naturally, effortlessly, he absorbed it and in the process

> The appropriate image of himself,
> So formed, became himself and he breathed
> The breath of another nature as his own.
>
> (CP 513)

His imagination takes form from reality, and in turn reality, "a nature still without a shape, / Except his own" (CP 514), takes form from his imagination. Self and not-self, poet and monster, man and weather, these are a few of the infinitely variable terms for the process Stevens calls "the universal intercourse," part of a duet or harmonizing between the invisible and the visible:

> the voice
> In the clouds serene and final, next
>
> The grunted breath serene and final,
> The imagined and the real, thought
>
> And the truth, Dichtung und Wahrheit, all
> Confusion solved, as in a refrain
>
> One keeps on playing year by year,
> Concerning the nature of things as they are.
>
> (CP 177)

This dialogue crowds Stevens' poems with contrasting pairs: man and woman, day and night, north and south, silence and music, green and blue, sun and moon. No interchange, however, except perhaps the sexual one, embodies the process of mutual fulfillment so naturally, organically, and aptly as the process of breathing.

One problem Stevens had with his early sketches for a church of the spirit was the inability of the light, sky, or cloud-cloister-porch to suggest the conflict which was for him at the heart of life. Another was the inevitable recalcitrance of an achieved structure. A building can change only if eternally in completion, as Stevens wished in "Architecture," or if constantly dilapidating, as he suggested in "The Sketch of the Ultimate Politician." If the chapel of breath is to stand for the way in which "two things of opposite natures seem to depend / On one another," it must also recognize that "this [process] is the origin of change" (CP 392). It does so easily, for breath is "that which is always beginning because it is part / Of that which is always beginning, over and over" (CP 530). Breath is ever new: we "breathe, breathe upon the centre of / The breath life's latest, thousand senses" (CP 264). Life's latest thousand senses are a center for the self and the not-self, since "sense" is both the self's method of perception and the significance construed from the not-self. It is not possible to say which forms or informs the other because, like breath, they flow in the constant change and interchange of the perceived and the perceiver. The chapel of breath joins space, here, and time, now: breath is architecture, or shaping, and "breathing is the beating of time" (CP 330).

As spirit in its root meaning is breath, salvation in its root meaning is health. The church promises salvation through the spirit, Stevens health through the processes symbolized by breath and breathing. The physical fact that breathing creates health is also, for Stevens, a divine force. The "health of air" we "inhale . . . / To our se-pulchral hollows" (CP 470) resurrects the entombed self. Breathing consummates our "love of the real" on which "we fling ourselves, constantly longing" (CP 470), and it is, for Stevens, salvation in many of its meanings: breathing saves us from the evil which is not living in a physical world, it preserves us from the suffocating iso-lation of the self which is death, it unites us with ultimate reality which, for Stevens, must include the physical,

and it is the agent or process of spiritual experience de-
termining the spirit's redemption. The chapel of breath
is for the believer, "St. Armorer's" summarizes, "the
origin and keep of its health and his own" (CP 530).

Finally, and importantly to a man who believed that
life is poetry, breath is the medium of speech. The
biblical "breath of life" (Genesis 2.7) made man a living
soul; poetic breath gives him intensest life. "Our breath,"
Stevens explains in "An Ordinary Evening in New
Haven," is "the origin of a mother tongue" (CP 470):

> the capable
> In the midst of foreignness, the syllable
> Of recognition, avowal, impassioned cry,
>
> The cry that contains its converse in itself,
> In which looks and feelings mingle and are part
> As a quick answer modifies a question.
> (CP 471)

We live, like Adam outside Eden, in a place not our
own and not ourselves, but we are not, like the Jew of
"Winter Bells," trapped. Poetry and poetic perception
do for us what religion did for John Zeller: they create
a home in the midst of foreignness, passion amidst bewilderment, affirmation amidst doubt.

As the breath of God is His life-giving essence, the
breath of the poet is creative imagination. The chapel
of breath which must, in the death of religion, replace
the deaf-mute church is the church of the spirit and
the temple of imagination. It is a return from created object to creating force, from the concept of God, which
is "only one of the things of the imagination" (LWS 369),

to imagination itself. The chapel of breath is "no sign of life but life, / Itself" (CP 529). In it, the man of imagination "walks and does as he lives and likes" (CP 530). His vibrant life is the merging of himself and his land; the sufficiency of that life, its radiance, creates health and speech. To turn from the deaf-mute church to the chapel of breath is to reach toward the source of all faiths: the creating power which for Stevens means life itself. To tell the Archbishop of Canterbury to jump off the end of the dock is to reaffirm life, to embrace doubt and change, and to be, in the glorious release of waving adieu, once again one's singular self.

❧ 3 ❧

A MYSTICAL THEOLOGY:
Stevens' Poetic Trinity

> The theory of poetry, that is to say, the total of the theories of poetry, often seems to become in time a mystical theology.
>
> (NA 173)

STEVENS wrote poetry for several reasons: to formulate his ideas and relate himself to the world (LWS 306), to discover a value that suffices (LWS 345), to provide a sanction for life (LWS 600), to give imagination variety (OP 221) through "a fresh conception of the world" (LWS 590), and, finally, for the "mystical motive" cited in "The Irrational Element in Poetry," "to find God" (OP 221). Though he protested that "the last thing in the world that [he] should want to do would be to formulate a system" (LWS 864), his theory of poetry did in time become a mystical theology. His mind could not help formulating systems: systematic about color, about the seasons, about sun and moon, man and woman, Stevens is also systematic in his attempt to find God. Implicit in his mystical theology is a poetic trinity which, though never thrust upon us fully formulated, can be deduced from his elaborations on the statement that "God and the imagination are one" (LWS 701): if imagination is God, poetry is its emanation and the poet, of imagination all compact, is its incarnation.

"Theology" seems a strange term for the poetry and poetic theory of a man who scoffed at the Herr Doktors

82

of the church and dismissed Aquinas, in the poem "Les Plus Belles Pages," as an "automaton, in logic self-contained" (CP 245). This poem, Stevens commented, stresses that although Aquinas is "of great modern interest," his theology, as such, is not (OP 294). It is not of interest for the familiar reason that it is a structure of ideas no longer relevant to the structure of things, because it is self-contained or, in the poem's metaphors, because it is moonlight without the milkman. Aquinas himself, however, is of interest: "A Collect of Philosophy" presents him as a man who was committed to the "inherently poetic" idea that all existence flows from God (OP 188), an idea with which the modern poet must also grapple. Structures of ideas are necessary and specifically, for Stevens, structures of ideas about God are necessary. The struggle of the modern poet, he repeatedly insists, is "to create something as valid as the idea of God has been, and for that matter remains" (LWS 435). To do this, modern poetry must incorporate theology: the investigation of the nature of God and of His relation to the world. The poet's theology, however, will be theology salvaged from the self-containment which once diminished it. It will be a "theology after breakfast," one which "sticks to the eye" (CP 245): a theology improved by poetry's stubborn adherence to the ordinary world. The poet as a theologian after breakfast can, Stevens believed, establish the mystical theology of his poetry as "immeasurably a greater thing than religion" (OP 166).

Stevens did not balk at the equation of poet and theologian, but the equation of poet and mystic made him nervous. He usually introduced and fortified the subject with references to thinkers like Brémond (OP 221) and Bergson (NA 49), and he often shrank from its implications, conceding, for example, that the theory "sounds a bit like sacerdotal jargon" (NA 174), insisting that "it is not a question of making saints out of poets" (NA 51), and confessing that "it can lie in the temperament of very few of us to write poetry in order to find God" (OP 222). Nevertheless, Stevens returned again and again to the subject, each time emphasizing that poetry is mystical: that it has a spiritual meaning neither apparent to the senses nor obvious to reason alone and that it relates to or results from an individual's direct communication with what might hesitantly be called ultimate reality.

The intensity of experience which Bergson attributes to the founder of religion, the mystic, and the saint, Stevens attributes to the poet. "The experience of the poet is," he writes, "of no less degree than the experience of the mystic and we may be certain that in the case of poets, the peers of saints, those experiences are of no less a degree than the experiences of the saints themselves" (NA 50-51). The equation of poet and mystic, like that of poet and theologian, is possible because for Stevens the idea of God is and always has been "the major poetic idea in the world" (LWS 378). The thinker of this idea—the founder of religion, the saint, or the mystic—is by definition also the poet. Poet and mystic share a method, the imaginative resistance to chaos, an end, the apprehension of the harmonious and orderly, and a resultant liberation, the ecstasy available through imaginative vision.

The imagination is the force which moves through chaos to order, through dissonance to harmony, through the evil which is for Stevens unassimilated reality to the good of imaginative integration. "The poet who wishes to contemplate the good in the midst of confusion is," therefore, "like the mystic who wishes to contemplate

God in the midst of evil" (OP 225): both press back against the pressures of contemporary reality with the force of imagination. As the method is similar, so is the end: the mystic defies confusion through God, and the poet resists it through finding "the good which, in the Platonic sense, is synonymous with God . . . the good in what is harmonious and orderly" (OP 222). This apprehension of the harmonious, whether of God or simply of order, creates ecstasy, a state of elevation which Stevens attributes to both the mystic and the poet and which he defines, tentatively, as "the feeling of deliverance, of a release, of a perfection touched, of a vocation so that all men may know the truth and that the truth may set them free" (NA 51). At each point, the experience shared is the working of imagination.

To incorporate theology into poetry, to transfer the experience of the mystic to the poet, and to apply to poetry the promise of Jesus—"ye shall know the truth, and the truth shall make you free" (John 8.32)—is characteristic of Stevens' search for a substitute for religion. He is consistent, careful, and above all conservative, for his philosophy stresses established institutions, prefers gradual development to abrupt change, and aims at selective preservation rather than hasty, if thorough, destruction. If he could be called a radical, it is only in the etymological sense, for his method is always to strip away accretions and expose the source worth preservation and development. Capitalism, for instance, Stevens judges worth preserving if seized at its source and made "up-to-date" (LWS 292). Similarly, imagination he found "not worthy to survive if it is to be identified with the romantic," that is, as he indicates in context, the sentimental; however, if we can "somehow cleanse the imag-

ination of the romantic," it will be again "one of the
great human powers . . . the only genius" (NA 138-139,
see also LWS 277).

What holds for economic and poetic institutions holds
also for established religious institutions. "No one," Stevens declared, "believes in the church as an institution
more than I do" (LWS 348). He wanted to preserve it
by returning it to what "Notes toward a Supreme Fiction" terms a first idea. "If you take the varnish and dirt
of generations off a picture," Stevens explained, "you see
it in its first idea. If you think about the world without
its varnish and dirt, you are a thinker of the first idea"
(LWS 426-427). The church cleansed of centuries of ac-
cumulated dogma and ritual returns to the chapel of
breath: the active, creating, fluid force which once in-
formed it. Theology cleared of its outdated theoretical
structure becomes concrete, constructive thought about
God and His relation to the world. The idea of God
Himself, finally, if the theological fabrications which
have come to surround Him are swept away, can be
recognized as "only one of the things of the imagination"
(LWS 369) and we can deify the source itself: imagination.

This conservative habit of mind helps to explain why
in Stevens' poetry and ruminations on poetry imagination
becomes a three-personed God: a secular trinity. His
mind gravitates naturally toward established institutions
that might be purified and thereby preserved, and the
trinity was no exception. It is necessary to stress, however, that Stevens never codified his mystical theology.
Shy of anything resembling dogma, he suggests rather
than states, using imagery to evoke tentative comparisons
and mustering all the resources of what Helen Vendler

calls his "pensive style"—explicit or implicit qualification, conditional propositions, questions, appositions, and meditations on the words "seem" and "as if"[1]—to avoid final assertions. To puzzle out his trinity is an occupation as exacting as, for Eliot, the effort to comprehend Incarnation: one pursues "hints and guesses, / Hints followed by guesses."[2] There are numerous hints and plausible guesses, however, for in Stevens' poetry the imagination assumes many of the attributes of God: it is the still point and center of transformations, the father proclaimed by the heavens, the source of holiness, innocence, and beatitude, the enthroned and creative Word. Immanent in the world, the imagination in Stevens' imagery becomes the indwelling dove or its secular, urban equivalent, the pigeon. Incarnated, it becomes Stevens' hero, the deliverer who is born in winter and heralded by a star, the savior who brings a supreme fiction or Logos, wakes us to truth, suffers with and for us, mediates between us and ultimate reality, and, finally, promises the faithful a continuous rebirth through imagination.

Before discussing these transformations separately and in detail, it is important to consider three of Stevens' habits of mind which helped to make the creation of a secular deity, or even trinity, inevitable: his constant personification and search for a Person in nature, his direct desire to make poetry a substitute for religion, and the triadic form his quest for order often assumes. That personification is characteristic of both poetry and religion would delight Stevens, for it is further proof of his theory

[1] *On Extended Wings*, p. 13. For a full discussion of this method, see her first chapter, "The Pensive Man: The Pensive Style," pp. 13-37.

[2] *Complete Poems and Plays*, p. 136.

that poetic and religious thought are one. As the poet attributes human qualities or feelings to nonhuman organisms, objects, or abstract ideas, so the Christian gives anthropomorphic form to many of his religious abstractions. Each personification, poetic or religious, is at once a kind of man and a kind of idea. Stevens' poetry is filled with personifications, and through them, as pointed out by Frank Doggett, he "gains for his large abstractions something of the urgency and poignancy belonging to individual lives."[3] They give his poetry power, concentration, and, frequently, added playfulness or solemnity. Often, like the aphorism, they are the core from which the poem develops. The Paltry Nude, Infanta Marina, Vincentine, and So-and-So, Puella Parvula, Madame La Fleurie, and the Interior Paramour are personified abstractions which range from the goddess of spring to the muse of imagination. The Brave Man, the Sleight-of-Hand Man, the Snow Man, the Silent Man, and the Large Red Man incarnate qualities ranging through sun, earth, and nothingness to imagination itself. These are artificial confections, products, like So-and-So, of a craftsman's skill, but they signal a habit of mind which came to Stevens from his earliest youth and emerged in a constant search for a Person who might be to nature what the personification is to the poem: a controlling center, an embodiment of meaning.

"I wish," Stevens sighed in 1906, "that groves still *were* sacred—or, at least, that something was" (LWS 86). In his young manhood, whimsy and aestheticism led him to fancy a fairy behind every bush, so that "the first clucking of the wood-frogs," for instance, ". . . sounded like

---

[3] "This Invented World: Stevens' 'Notes Toward a Supreme Fiction,'" *ELH*, 28 (September 1961), 285.

the creaking of Flora's wain" (LWS 70) and in the blue
of twilight it seemed that "any moment the fairies might
light their lamps" (LWS 72). The wish, however, is not
pure fancy, for in the absence of any controlling center,
Stevens preferred something to nothing: thus, he demanded in 1902, "give me the fairies, the Cloud-Gatherer,
the Prince of Peace, the Mirror of Virtue" (LWS 60). The
Prince of Peace, traditionally an epithet for Christ, might
be a surprise in the list, but he is not altogether different
from the fairies: he is a spirit in nature, something to make
the slovenly wilderness come alive with meaning. God,
of course, is the supreme example of these attributes, and
Stevens could never bring himself totally to reject God.
"I do not understand," he wrote Elsie in 1909, "that
[doubters] deny God. I think everyone admits that in
some form or other.—The thought makes the world
sweeter—even if God be no more than the mystery of
Life" (LWS 140). Two years before his death, Stevens
felt the same hesitant willingness to believe. "At my age,"
he wrote Thomas McGreevy, "it would be nice to be
able to read more and think more and be myself more
and to make up my mind about God, say, before it is too
late, or at least before he makes up his mind about me"
(LWS 763).

Stevens was always preoccupied with God, and one of
the central problems his poetic theory confronts is the
"some form or other" that God must take if poetry is to
become, as religion once was, a supreme fiction. Santayana's *Interpretations of Poetry and Religion* (1900)
provides a background for this second habit of mind:
Stevens' conviction that poetry must subsume concerns
hitherto confined to religion. Samuel French Morse suggests that Stevens, as editor of the Harvard *Advocate* and

friend of the philosopher, anonymously reviewed *Interpretations of Poetry and Religion* soon after its appearance, but whether or not he reviewed it, he surely read it
and found there, as Morse surmises, "the embodiment of
the poetic doctrine he was looking for."[4]

Santayana's thesis is that poetry and religion can and
should be identical. As the *Advocate* reviewer summarizes, "both religion and poetry appeal to the imagination
rather than to the understanding. Their function is not to
discover and describe new facts of experience, but rather
to remould and interpret data already given by science
and reflection."[5] Both, that is, have to do with the world
of values, appreciations, and ideals. They have been differentiated, Santayana argued, by their effect on the
practical world of affairs: "Poetry is called religion when
it intervenes in life, and religion, when it merely super-
venes upon life, is seen to be nothing but poetry."[6] They
need not be differentiated, however, since in the ideal
they are one. Santayana maintained that "poetry raised to
its highest power is identical with religion grasped in its
utmost truth; at their point of union both reach their
utmost purity and beneficence, for then poetry loses its
frivolity and ceases to demoralize, while religion surren-
ders its illusions and ceases to deceive."[7] This point of
union is the ideal Stevens has in mind in his essays when
he rejects the "minor wish-fulfillments" of frivolous poetry (NA 139) and when he huffs, "to the man who is

---

[4] *Wallace Stevens: Poetry as Life* (New York: Pegasus, 1970),
p. 55.

[5] Quoted in Morse, *Poetry as Life*, p. 54.

[6] *Interpretations of Poetry and Religion* (New York: Charles
Scribner's Sons, 1900), p. v.

[7] *Interpretations of Poetry and Religion*, p. 290.

seeking the sanction of life in poetry, the namby-pamby is an intolerable dissipation" (NA 173).

Poetry for Santayana and Stevens was anything but the namby-pamby. Though their poems could be light and jesting, they claimed for poetry in general a strong, decisive, and relevant role. *Interpretations of Poetry and Religion*, Daniel Fuchs emphasizes, "embodies what Santayana considered a necessity for relevant poetry—the element of prophecy. For Santayana, the poet must either express an existing religion or herald one which he believes possible."[8] Unable to express the faith of the deaf-mute church, Stevens took with the utmost seriousness the responsibility for heralding a new faith. "As scepticism becomes both complete and profound," he wrote, "we face either a true civilization or a blank; and literature ought to be one of the factors to determine the choice. Certainly, if civilization is to consist only of man himself, and it is, the arts must take the place of divinity, at least as a stage in whatever general principle or progress is involved" (LWS 564). Literature, then, is crucial to the progress of civilization. The general principle involved is the evolution of a new divinity, the embodiment of a new ideal, and this is poetry's strength. Divinity is the postulate of what Santayana calls "poetry raised to its highest power." Poetry must consider God, for whether or not He is a verifiable fact, He is an essential ideal. The *Advocate* review, therefore, discards the question of God's existence "as an independent absolute *thing*, an object, so to speak, for scientific exploration" and asserts that "He assuredly exists as a necessary postulate of the

[8] "Wallace Stevens and Santayana," in *Patterns of Commitment in American Literature*, ed. Marston Lafrance (Toronto: Univ. of Toronto Press, 1967), p. 144.

poetic imagination, embodying in concrete form the per-
fected projection of life, which alone can satisfy the
will."[9]

If Stevens did write this review, he certainly had not
changed his mind forty years later when he drew up a
memorandum for a Chair of Poetry at Harvard. He
wrote his friend Henry Church, who was to endow the
chair, that

> while aesthetic ideas are commonplaces in this field,
> its import is not the import of the superficial. The
> major poetic idea in the world is and always has been
> the idea of God. One of the visible movements of the
> modern imagination is the movement away from the
> idea of God. The poetry that created the idea of
> God will either adapt it to our different intelligence,
> or create a substitute for it, or make it unnecessary.
>
> (LWS 377-378)

"These alternatives," Stevens admitted, "probably mean
the same thing" (LWS 378), for the creation of a new god
is the automatic supersession of the old, but his major
emphasis is that any poetry worthy of the name must
consider God. The essay "A Collect of Philosophy,"
written eleven years later, rounds out Stevens' plan for
the Chair of Poetry by listing, as in a syllabus, the themes
for the supreme poetry of the future. These "central
doctrines," which he cites in the phrases of Paul Weiss,
include: "all beings have at least a trace of God in them,"
"all existence is owed to God," and "all things are in
God" (OP 188).

[9] Quoted in Morse, *Life as Poetry*, p. 55.

Stevens' conviction that poetry must create and herald a fully satisfying substitute for religion, then, combined with his habit of personification to make it philosophically and personally imperative that his poetry become a theology. The shape of this theology might have been influenced by a third habit of mind: Stevens' tendency toward triadic forms. "A triad," R. P. Blackmur insists in an essay on Stevens, "makes a trinity, and a trinity, to a certain kind of poetic imagination, is the only tolerable form of unity."[10] Stevens had this kind of imagination.

His poems from the beginning often had a cast of trios or a triadic title. The early "Plot against the Giant," for instance, pits three temptresses against the poet's senses of smell, sight, and hearing. It is "three travelers" (OP 127) who watch a sunrise in his first play: "three figures" (OP 132) like "three dead men" (OP 133) to balance the play's "three beggars" (OP 139), the girl, her father, and her dead lover. Stevens' late and intense "mythology of modern death" (CP 435), "The Owl in the Sarcophagus," creates three mystical figures—two brothers, "high sleep" and "high peace," and the mysterious third form, "she that says / Good-by in the darkness" (CP 431)—and one of his very last poems, published a year before his death, is a final "Conversation with Three Women of New England" (OP 108). Stevens' poems deal as well with the triads of things or ideas that frequently form their titles. These are sometimes for emphasis, as in "No Possum, No Sop, No Taters" (CP 293), but more often they plot the contention of three things or ideas, of "Wild Ducks,

[10] "Wallace Stevens: An Abstraction Blooded," in *Form and Value in Modern Poetry* (Garden City, N.Y.: Doubleday, 1952), p. 213.

People and Distances" (cp 328) or of "Forces, the Will &
the Weather" (cp 228). He seems to think in threes.

It is not surprising, then, to find that Stevens prefers
to write in a three-line stanza, from its beginnings in the
earliest poems like "The Snow Man," "Another Weeping
Woman," and "The Doctor of Geneva" to its perfection
in all the major late poems: "Notes toward a Supreme
Fiction," "The Auroras of Autumn," "The Owl in the
Sarcophagus," "An Ordinary Evening in New Haven,"
and "The Rock." The form fits the content, which
Glauco Cambon calls "the triadic movement . . . in so
many typical poems of Stevens."[11] Though he sometimes
indulges in thirteen ways of looking, Stevens is more
often

> of three minds,
> Like a tree
> In which there are three blackbirds.
>
> (cp 92)

In "Theory," therefore, he gives three examples, in "So-
and-So" three projections, and in "The Idea of Order at
Key West," as Riddel points out, "three realities: sea,
song, and the higher synthesis of the two, another repetition of Stevens' secular trinity."[12] On the highest level,
in "Notes toward a Supreme Fiction," he marks three
criteria for the ultimate poetry: abstraction, change, and
pleasure.

At critical moments of thought for Stevens, there are
almost always three projections to be considered. In
"Chocorua to Its Neighbor," for instance, he theorizes,

[11] *The Inclusive Flame: Studies in Modern American Poetry*
(Bloomington: Indiana Univ. Press, 1965), p. 99.
[12] *Clairvoyant Eye*, p. 119.

To say more than human things with human voice,
That cannot be; to say human things with more
Than human voice, that, also, cannot be;
To speak humanly from the height or from the depth
Of human things, that is acutest speech.

(CP 300)

In an almost parallel construction from "The Auroras of Autumn," he finds that "a happy people in an unhappy world— / It cannot be," nor is "a happy people in a happy world" right; the true proposition is the third: "an unhappy people in a happy world" (CP 420). If the characters, titles, lines, and propositions often came to him in threes, it is partly because, as "Credences of Summer" confirms, the very process of the imagination itself is trinitarian:

Three times the concentred self takes hold, three times
The thrice concentred self, having possessed

The object, grips it in savage scrutiny,
Once to make captive, once to subjugate
Or yield to subjugation, once to proclaim
The meaning of the capture, this hard prize,
Fully made, fully apparent, fully found.

(CP 376)

A trinity seemed for Stevens the most tolerable form of unity, and when the hardest prize of all, the idea of God, was fully made or fully found, it also was likely to be a trinity.

Stevens' poetic trinity was both found and made. Its contours are those found in the faith of St. Armorer's

Church, but it is made for the chapel of breath, for a faith which deifies imagination. Like other of Stevens' trans-valuations, his poetic trinity is "a sacred syllable rising from sacked speech" (CP 530), the speech of Christianity. The word "sacked" is apt, for it implies both the helpless-ness of the victim and the strength of the conqueror who appropriates what is valuable and leaves the dross behind. Stevens' work with the trinity is, then, twofold: it is a critique of the old forms and a construction of new ones. In considering Stevens' poetic equivalents for God, the Holy Ghost, and Christ, the rest of this chapter will com-pare each old and new form and then trace for each its various and developing manifestations in his poetry.

Stevens' critique of God has three major thrusts: as a wish-fulfilling projection of the human on the nonhuman, God is a confusion of two distinct realms; as a dogmatic concept, He is constantly outdated; as a ruling power, He usurps the prerogatives belonging rightfully to the imag-ination. The origin of the gods is, for Stevens, the same as the origin of a child's imaginary playmate. "Is it," he asks, with every appearance of believing that it is, "one of the normal activities of humanity, in the solitude of reality and in the unworthy treatment of solitude, to create com-panions, a little colossal . . . who, if not superficially ex-plicative, are, at least, assumed to be full of the secret of things?" (OP 207-208). These companions take our shape, since they are, like God, "a postulate of the ego" (OP 171), "the centre of the pathetic fallacy" (LWS 444), or "simply a projection of itself by a race of egoists, which it is natural for them to treat as sacred" (LWS 349). They share our nationality, so that "the gods of China," for instance, "are always Chinese" (OP 211), and they share our virtues and faults, so that though perhaps "a noble people" can "evolve a noble God" (OP 174), more often, "since men made the world, the inevitable god is the beggar" (OP 171).

This transferal is natural, if somewhat pathetic, but it is also dangerous, for it falsifies the inhuman and weakens the human. By projecting our image upon the universe, we arrogate to ourselves its creation and government. This involves the same ignorant and fallacious condescension which attributes human thought to a pet, since through our deities we make the universe "an intelligence, / Like a widow's bird / Or an old horse" (CP 18). We must be humble enough to recognize the "muddy centre before we breathed" (CP 383), the essence which precedes all human myths. "There is," Stevens insists in explicating this thought, "a huge abstraction, venerable and articulate and complete, that has no reference to us" (LWS 444). We must never tame this abstraction by giving it human form,

> Never suppose an inventing mind as source
> Of this idea nor for that mind compose
> A voluminous master folded in his fire.
>
> (CP 381)

To reject the human myth is suddenly to exist in "the remotest cleanliness of a heaven / That has expelled us and our images" (CP 381). It is suddenly to find ourselves complete in the immense and frightening freedom of a universe which is alien to us.

If this transferal is unfair to what is not ourselves, it is also debilitating to what is. Man imagining God is for Stevens like "Cinderella fulfilling herself beneath the roof" (CP 405). God as Prince Charming usurps not only

our better qualities but also our active ones, so that we
become daydreamers in rags. If only we would not pity
ourselves so much, Stevens feels,

> he would not pity us so much,
> Weaken our fate, relieve us of woe both great
> And small, a constant fellow of destiny,
>
> A too, too human god, self-pity's kin
> And uncourageous genesis.
>   (CP 315)

This self-pity is like a neurosis, for through it we make
impossible our assumption of full humanity and responsibility. On the one hand, we inflate the human form to
such a degree that we can never satisfy our projected ideal;
on the other, we give away our better qualities only to
leave ourselves dependent and debased.

Heaven with its administrative system is, for Stevens,
"the palais de justice of chambermaids" which "tops the
horizon with its colonnades." From it, as from a pompous
state capitol, come pronouncements so grand as to render
us in comparison silly and servile: "somehow the brave
dicta of its kings / Make more awry our faulty human
things" (CP 98). Rightly interpreted, as in the myth of
in-bar and ex-bar from "Esthétique du Mal," the posi-
tions are reversed and the gods become dependent upon
us. In-bar is the subjective self, the particular, "the actual,
the warm, the near," and ex-bar is the "clouds, benevo-
lences, distant heads" that compose "the golden forms /
And the damasked memory of the golden forms" (CP
317) which we once invested with our finer qualities.
In-bar and ex-bar, Riddel points out, are "another cri-

tique of religious anthropomorphism as a constrictive form of vital mythology. We must, [Stevens] implies, reclaim our humanity. . . . Before we can be 'wholly human,' we must replace the empty rites for abstract divinities with vital expressions of our selves, including our priceless faults."[13] The glory of the gods, Stevens says elsewhere, is "the fundamental glory of men and women, who being in need of it create it, elevate it, without too much searching of its identity" (OP 208). It is time, he feels, for men to relinquish what is not their own, the alien and abstract universe, and to reclaim the fundamental glory that is rightly theirs.

Stevens made several efforts to formulate a god who would be recognizably alien and abstract and would not, by competing unfairly with humanity, turn human things awry. His plea in "Less and Less Human, O Savage Spirit" is for the admission that "the human . . . has no cousin in the moon" (CP 328). If our old god was like the man-in-the-moon, the new must be neither cousin nor cartoon. "He must dwell quietly," Stevens stipulates, and "be incapable of speaking" (CP 327):

> If there must be a god in the house, let him be one
> That will not hear us when we speak: a coolness,
>
> A vermilioned nothingness, any stick of the mass
> Of which we are too distantly a part.
> (CP 328)

One solution might be to make our god out of the whole mass: the physical myth uncontaminated by the human

---

[13] "The Metaphysical Changes," p. 72.

myth. Out of the muddy center, therefore, Stevens pos-
tulated "a master of mud":

> The peach-bud maker,
> The mud master,
> The master of the mind.
>   (CP 148)

This is "time in its weather, our most sovereign lord"
(CP 332), the creative force in nature, but it is a savage
spirit so inhuman as almost to be irrelevant. *Owl's Clover*
suggests another solution: the deification of man's own
muddy center, human because essential to us but inhuman
when abstracted and generalized. Ananke, "the common
god" (OP 59), is, as Riddel suggests, "the final, the inner
god, 'who ordains / For races, not for men'; that is, he is
the human constant, the elemental need."[14] He is described in abstract theological terms which, as Helen
Vendler notes, borrow the paradoxes belonging to Je-
hovah and "the tone of the sterner Latin doxologies."[15]
He joins the Subman, "the man below the man below the
man" (OP 66), and the Sprawling Portent, which seems to
be the future moving through the heavens, to make an
odd trinity: Ananke the god above, the Subman the god
below, and the Portent manifesting them in the sky.

Ananke and the Subman are both attempts to deify
the essential quality of man. After the rhetorical debauch
of *Owl's Clover*, Stevens settled down to calmer, less
pretentious formulations of this quality. Aquinas "spoke, /
Kept speaking, of God," Stevens notes in "Les Plus Belles
Pages," "I changed the word to man" (CP 245). As he
wrote Renato Poggioli, his Italian translator, "The an-

---

[14] *Clairvoyant Eye*, p. 130.   [15] *On Extended Wings*, p. 97.

thropomorphic can only yield in the end to anthropos: God must in the end, in the life of the mind, yield to man."[16] Specifically, God yields to the quality in man which made God: the imaginative, the fictive power which, like beauty, is eternal in the flesh. The imagination is not a projection of itself by a race of egoists but the power by which we conceive the universe as a thing apart: it is "the music summoned by the birth / That separates us from the wind and sea" (CP 87). It does not set up a rigid and unattainable ideal because the imagination's "resemblances and . . . repetitions of resemblances" are fluid: they are "a source of the ideal" (NA 81) and they are also the force which makes it possible that "the ideal itself remains alive with an enormous life" (NA 82).

Stevens' second criticism of God, much like his criticism of the deaf-mute church, is that, as a dogmatic concept, He cannot remain alive with enormous life. First, deities are parochial, so that gods fashioned in Europe, for instance, have "no place / In Africa." In "The Greenest Continent," they are "like marble figures fallen, left / In the streets" (OP 58). Stevens stressed that "in trying to create something as valid as the idea of God has been . . . the first necessity seems to be breadth" (LWS 435). Imagination, as a universal, has this breadth, and in "The Greenest Continent," as he explained to Hi Simons, he had tried to show "that, if ideas of God are in conflict, the idea of pure poetry: imagination, extended beyond local consciousness, may be an idea to be held in common by South, West, North and East" (LWS 370). Unlike God, imagination has a jurisdiction without limits. Secondly, just as the gods cannot move in space, they cannot

[16] *Mattino Domenicale ed Altre Poesie*, trans. Poggioli (Torino: Guilio Einuadi, 1954), p. 180.

move in time. The juxtaposition of a seventeenth-century deity with a twentieth-century battlefield, for instance, is as ridiculous as it is sad:

> The Got whome we serve is able to deliver
> Us. Good chemistry, good common man, what
> Of that angelic sword? Creature of
> Ten times ten times dynamite, convulsive
> Angel, convulsive shatterer, gun,
> Click, click, the Got whom we serve is able,
> Still, still to deliver us.
>   (CP 273)

The Got and his believers are like the President of "Notes toward a Supreme Fiction"[17] who "ordains the bee to be / Immortal" while all around chaos and change reign in glory:

> And the banners of the nation flutter, burst
> On the flag-poles in a red-blue dazzle, whack
> At the halyards.
>   (CP 390)

Imagination, in contrast, is at home in "this dizzle-dazzle of being new" (CP 530). It can never be outmoded because, like the bee, it is always, to use Stevens' pun, "an inexhaustible being" (CP 390).

Stevens' third and most important point of criticism is that God pretends to be what imagination in fact is: all-seeing, all-powerful, and all-loving. "Negation," a poem

---

[17] Eugene Paul Nassar suggests that the President in "Notes" is "a satiric figure for all the gods the transcendentalists have created" (*Wallace Stevens: An Anatomy of Figuration* [Philadelphia: Univ. of Pennsylvania Press, 1965], p. 199).

Morse terms "an almost Hardyesque conceit,"[18] is a bitter indictment of a creator who is "blind," "incapable," and at best indifferent, at worst cruel. "Struggling toward his harmonious whole" (CP 97), he rejects the imperfect and the human, and

> For this, then, we endure brief lives,
> The evanescent symmetries
> From that meticulous potter's thumb.
> (CP 98)

The poem's title refers most obviously to its overt denial or negation of the Christian God, but it hints also that God Himself is a negation: a false concept, a nonentity, something absent. A negation is, in a third meaning, the opposite of something positive, and the poem, as a negation of a negation, implies this positive: the doctrine of the imagination which is vision, capableness, and love.

"God is in me," Stevens maintained, "or else is not at all (does not exist)" (OP 172). This indwelling deity is in-bar, the subjective self, the divinity within, which, like Canon Aspirin, chooses to include "the whole, / The complicate, the amassing harmony" (CP 403). It is the imaginative receptivity, helplessly open to "all pleasures and all pains":

> Passions of rain, or moods in falling snow;
> Grievings in loneliness, or unsubdued
> Elations when the forest blooms; gusty
> Emotions on wet roads on autumn nights.
> (CP 67)

[18] " 'Lettres d'un Soldat,' " *Dartmouth College Library Bulletin*, n.s., 4 (December 1961), 47.

This unsubdued responsiveness is, like the action of breathing, the mutually sustaining and modifying interchange of self and environment, invisible and visible, imagination and reality. It is a yoking of stimulus and reply: rain and passion, bloom and elation. The first requirement for imagination is that it touch reality with the depth and inclusiveness of vision which the blind God of "Negation" lacks. Imaginative vision is the very faculty of sight and insight, the ability to perceive nature and to respond sensitively. It looks outward to conceive the world and inward to conceive the self, and in its doubleness, it is both an eye and an I. It is all-seeing in that it encompasses for Stevens all there is: the objective world and the subjective world.

The God of "Negation" is inadequate because he is a "too vague idealist" (CP 98), problematically an eye without an I. This is for Stevens not only undesirable but impossible. That "the eye's plain version" of a thing— reportorial vision without the subjective elaboration of "an and yet, and yet, and yet" (CP 465)—is not sight is the point of Stevens' "Poem Written at Morning." To concentrate solely on the eye's objective catalogue, as God in his omniscience is purported to do, is to divide the thing from its self or essence, which is what the wobbling, hedging subjective self feels about it and which can be expressed by the imagination, by metaphor and by its resemblances, alone. "The truth must be," therefore,

> That you do not see, you experience, you feel,
> That the buxom eye brings merely its element
> To the total thing.
>
> (CP 219)

The God of "Negation" is like Kurt Vonnegut's God the Utterly Indifferent: he claims to see without experiencing or feeling. Because he is blank consciousness or an eye without an I, however, he cannot see, and he is a victim of the reductive experience described in "Notes toward a Supreme Fiction." Things for him are

> Not to be realized because not to
> Be seen, not to be loved nor hated because
> Not to be realized.
>   (CP 385)

Imaginative vision is conception, the giving of reality or life to what is seen. To make something real is to add to its objective outline our experience and feeling. Seeing brings realization and realization automatically entails loving or hating, the fullness of experience promised to the woman of "Sunday Morning" and denied, by His very nature, to God.

God's omniscience can be accuracy because it is indifference, but accuracy for Stevens is an unworthy and, in fact, an impossible, aim. Imaginative vision adds to things, "if only imagined but imagined well," the "false flick, false form, but falseness close to kin" that brings them to life. Things seen, therefore,

> must be visible or invisible,
> Invisible or visible or both:
> A seeing and unseeing in the eye.
>   (CP 385)

It is the unseeing in the eye, the experience and feeling which informs the eye's report, that the Captain of "The

Revolutionists Stop for Orangeade," like the God of "Negation," denies when he asks his men to be undeviating and accurate, "to sing standing in the sun." We are, like the soldiers, pitifully human: "hairy-backed and hump-armed, / Flat-ribbed and big-bagged" (CP 102). For us, omniscience is a myth. Though we may be wrong, under a "helmet without reason," we are all-seeing in that we are, at our best, all-feeling. Our song is our emotion,

> the vent of pity,
> Deeper than a truer ditty
> Of the real that wrenches,
> Of the quick that's wry.
> (CP 103)

The real that wrenches and is wry is unavailable to God; it is gloriously ours because imagination is the Utterly Caring, the all-seeing, the god within which is vision.

Just as imagination is all-seeing while God is blind, it is all-powerful while God is incapable. Stevens' conception of imagination's godlike power goes beyond the traditional Renaissance analogy between the poet and God, the Supreme Maker. He is not saying that imaginative power is like God's power and therefore worthy. Instead, he argues, imagination is the master of the powers falsely given to God: it is "the power of the mind over the possibilities of things" (NA 136), and, as such, it creates, rules, and restores the world. Because for Stevens imagination is indwelling, "the universe," as Ralph J. Mills points out, "receives its structure from within, not by the will of an external and omnipotent

God";[19] with this difference, however, imagination assumes the ends and means generally ascribed to God. Like God, it creates *ex nihilo*: without imagination, the earth is without form, void and dark, but imagination moving over earth brings forth "things seen and unseen, created from nothingness, / The heavens, the hells, the worlds, the longed-for lands" (CP 486). The agent of creation is the word—man's, not God's. The word defines and shapes each individual thing it touches, and joined in the integrative vision of poetry, words create a universe.

"A poet's words," Stevens affirms, "are of things that do not exist without the words" (NA 32): they have power over the possibilities of things because they lift them from potentiality into actuality. Words determine the aspect of the thing we are to see and the all-important nexus of resemblances by which we must evaluate it. "The power of literature," Stevens insists again and again, "is that in describing the world it creates what it describes. Those things that are not described do not exist" (LWS 495). Thus it is that

> the theory of description matters most.
> It is the theory of the word for those
>
> For whom the word is the making of the world,
> The buzzing world and lisping firmament.
> (CP 345)

The buzzing world is a world slipping always toward chaos, and it is the word alone that through description

---

[19] "The Image of the Rock," rpt. in *Critical Essays*, ed. Borroff, p. 100.

brings the external scene within the control of the individual sensibility.

Words bring forth things; poems, or articulated collections of words, bring forth worlds. "The poem," as Stevens defined it in the "Adagia," "is a nature created by the poet" (OP 166), and the poet's words, as "Effects of Analogy" explains, "have made a world that transcends the world and a life livable in that transcendence" (NA 130). This was not mere rhetoric, for when Stevens surveyed his collected work, he was, like God, "glad," and he called it "the planet on the table" (CP 532). In it he found, "word for word, / The poem that took the place of a mountain," an actual place that he had created, entered, and experienced:

> he had recomposed the pines,
> Shifted the rocks and picked his way among clouds,
>
> For the outlook that would be right,
> Where he would be complete in an unexplained
> completion.
>   (CP 512)

The truly sufficing poem for Stevens, as Babette Deutsch points out, is "to the region we inhabit what the universe might be to God":[20] the planet, the mountain, the world that transcends the world, all our quirky imaginative creations, are real and can be called good. "We enjoy the ithy oonts and long-haired / Plomets," Stevens re-

---

[20] *Poetry in Our Time: A Critical Survey of Poetry in the English-speaking World, 1900 to 1960*, 2nd ed. (Garden City, N.Y.: Doubleday, 1963), p. 285.

capitulated with a jab at his antiquated rival, "as the Herr Gott / Enjoys his comets" (CP 349).

Imagination not only creates and enjoys but also rules and restores the world. Since nothing is fixed—"nothing solid is its solid self" (CP 345)—creation must be the continual emergence of order out of chaos. Imagination is the jar which conquers every slovenly wilderness. Over the wind, the clouds, the "trembling trees," and "the water wallows / Of a vacant sea"—"over all these," Stevens summarizes, "the mighty imagination triumphs / Like a trumpet" (CP 456). It is not "God which always causeth us to triumph" (II Corinthians 2.14) but the imagination, which includes, as Mills contends, "man's innate ability to renew the world."[21] Its action is continual resurrection, and its power can restore even the vast desolation of World War II. The late poem "Imago" offers to supplement the Marshall Plan with "the imagination's hymns" and "the imagination's mercies." Its certitude of statement parallels in simplicity a nursery rhyme or a prayer:

> Who can pick up the weight of Britain,
> Who can move the German load
> Or say to the French here is France again?
> Imago. Imago. Imago.
> (CP 439)

Imagination is not, like the God of "Negation," an "incapable master" (CP 97). It is what men pretend God to be: the creating, ruling, restoring force which is "a light,

[21] "The Image of the Rock," rpt. in *Critical Essays*, ed. Borroff, p. 101.

a power, the miraculous influence" (CP 524) everywhere on earth.

If a God Who is all-seeing and all-powerful must, not to seem arbitrary and remote, also be all-loving, a God Who is blind, incompetent, and intolerant,

> Struggling toward his harmonious whole,
> Rejecting intermediate parts,
> Horrors and falsities and wrongs
> (CP 97)

can provoke only scorn mingled with fear. Traditionally, the Christian God is Himself love, and He provokes in men a "perfect love" which "casteth out fear" (I John 4.18). Christian love, according to I John 4, has three aspects: God's love for earth, the brotherhood emerging from our love in God for all men, and, finally, our love for God Himself. Imagination, which is all-seeing and all-powerful, is also for Stevens all-loving in each of these aspects. Its love, moreover, has an intensity that God's benevolence could never attain.

Stevens' early poem "Cy Est Pourtraicte, Madame Ste Ursule, et Les Unze Mille Vierges" flirts with blasphemy, for in it, God, seeing the virgin in His garden, quivers with a feeling "not heavenly love, / Or pity" (CP 22). Heavenly love is kindness, generosity, and the disposition to do good: it is not intense longing. The imagination's love, embodied in fallible men, is concrete and complex. Imagination is to the earth what God longs to be to Ursula: a lover. It is "the interior paramour" (CP 524) or "the lover that lies within us" (CP 394) full with love of "the earth, / Seen as inamorata" (CP 484). Constant, consuming, intense, and attentive,

Love of the real

Is soft in three-four cornered fragrances
From five-six cornered leaves, and green, the signal
To the lover, and blue, as of a secret place

In the anonymous color of the universe.
                    (CP 470)

The intensity of this love banishes anonymity in men as
in the earth. Through imagination comes brotherhood,
for imagination is the power by which we perceive resemblances among men as among things. It creates sympathy, the emotional and intellectual accord by which
we know that whatever affects us affects others similarly.
We are "true sympathizers," and in this, not in God, "so
great a unity, that it is bliss, / Ties us to those we love"
(CP 317). As our love for men is supposed to be the
image of the perfect love we feel for God, brotherhood
is for Stevens the image of the consuming love we feel
for the imagination itself, "of diviner love the day / And
flame and summer and sweet fire" (CP 87). "And for
what," Stevens asks in the invocation to "Notes toward
a Supreme Fiction," "except for you, do I feel love?"
Love for imagination is love for all there is. Imagination
is the force at "the central of our being"—from it we
emerge to seek intimacy with earth and sympathy with
men; within it we find "the vivid transparence that . . .
is peace" (CP 380).

In Stevens' formulations, the fictive power gradually
assumes not only God's rights and prerogatives but also
his robes and symbols. The divinity within of "Sunday
Morning" and the muse of "To the One of Fictive Mu-

sic" share a suggestive religiosity but no definite form. "The Man with the Blue Guitar" embodies this divinity in "the amorist Adjective aflame" (cp 172). "The initial letter of the word *Adjective*," as Frank Doggett points out, is "capitalized as though it were the name of a deity." The deity is love manifested in what Doggett aptly terms "the blue flame of individual consciousness ablaze with uprushing experience."[22] But it is in the late poetry, especially in "The Auroras of Autumn," "A Primitive like an Orb," and "An Ordinary Evening in New Haven," that imagination specifically takes the shape traditionally given God the Father. Perhaps prompted by Shelley, who defined imagination, in a phrase Stevens quotes, as "that imperial faculty whose throne is curtained within the invisible nature of man" (na 44), Stevens enthrones the fictive power in the invisible reaches of space. Space, as always, is psychic for Stevens—"our nature," he wrote, "is an illimitable space through which the intelligence moves without coming to an end" (na 53)—and dominating space, as the imagination dominates the mind, is the father or cosmic imagination of "Auroras":

> Master O master seated by the fire
> And yet in space and motionless and yet
> Of motion the ever-brightening origin.
>
> (cp 414)

He is associated with the fire which, as early as "Martial Cadenza," symbolizes life and consciousness—he is "a father bearded in his fire" (cp 438), a giant "crested /

[22] *Stevens' Poetry of Thought* (Baltimore: Johns Hopkins Press, 1966), p. 137.

With every prodigal, familiar fire" (CP 442)—and his throne is the still point, "the centre of transformations that / Transform for transformation's self" (CP 363). The "imagination that sits enthroned" (CP 417) is proclaimed by "the trumpet of morning" which "cries / This is the successor of the invisible" (CP 376); the heavens "adorn / And proclaim it" (CP 417) as a source of holiness and innocence (CP 418). The "strength at the centre" is "like blessed beams from out a blessed bush" (CP 477): it is, in Stevens' final formulations, God Himself, the divine flame lighting and consuming reality to reveal its power, radiance, and pervading glory.

At the same time that Stevens was deifying the imagination, he came more and more to imagine a deity beyond and behind the human imagination. "The very power of artistic creation," as James Benzinger explains, "will itself suggest, as it did to Kant and his followers and to Coleridge, the existence of some analogous power greater than itself." What Benzinger calls a "dim but tantalizing apprehension"[23] of this power glimmers through Stevens' essays and final poems. Since the poet, Stevens speculates in one essay, "shares the transformation, not to say apotheosis, accomplished by the poem . . . it must be this experience that teases him with that sense of the possibility of a remote, a mystical *vis* or *noeud vital*" (NA 49). Another essay particularizes this apprehension in the suggestion that the poet "comes to feel that his imagination is not wholly his own but that it may be part of a much larger, much more potent imagination, which it is his affair to try to get at" (NA 115).

[23] *Images of Eternity: Studies in the Poetry of Religious Vision, from Wordsworth to T. S. Eliot* (Carbondale: Southern Illinois Univ. Press, 1962), p. 239.

Although the remainder of the essay shuffles this theory aside as inconsonant with "that ultimate good sense which we term civilization" (NA 116), the intenser moments of Stevens' final poems return to a teasing sense of what he calls, in "To an Old Philosopher in Rome," "the celestial possible" (CP 509).

Though earlier poems suggest that there may be "an inhuman author" (CP 377) or "a single, certain truth" (CP 380), "Final Soliloquy of the Interior Paramour" and "Note on Moonlight" translate speculation into felt experience. In the "intensest rendezvous" of "Final Soliloquy" is the surge of beatitude, the moment when

> Here, now, we forget each other and ourselves.
> We feel the obscurity of an order, a whole,
> A knowledge, that which arranged the rendezvous.

Beyond individual imagination may be a greater imagination, a conceiving power or knowledge manifested in the unity of human experience and felt as "a warmth, / A light, a power, the miraculous influence" (CP 524). This influence, in "Note on Moonlight," allows the poet to make his peace with God. Here, as Benzinger points out, "the universe is again apprehended as religion and idealistic philosophy had apprehended it . . . as a pre-established harmony."[24] In its tranquil conviction, Stevens' confession seems almost Wordsworthian:

> So, then, this warm, wide, weatherless quietude
> Is active with a power, an inherent life,
>
> In spite of the mere objectiveness of things
> (CP 531)

[24] *Images of Eternity*, p. 241.

and there is, he continues, regaining his skepticism for
only a moment,

                        a purpose, empty
Perhaps, absurd perhaps, but at least a purpose,
Certain and ever more fresh. Ah! Certain, for sure . . .

                                        (CP 532)

The implications of his theory that God and the imagination are one must have surprised Stevens, for they led him
through a radical critique of God and through his hu-
manistic relegation of God's power to man's imagination
into a final, if hesitant, sense that there is a force and a
purpose which quickens, informs, and ennobles both man
and the universe.

The presence of God in man, in the world, and in the
church—God as He operates within reality—is traditionally called the Holy Ghost or Paraclete, from the Greek
Paraklētos, meaning Comforter or Advocate. "The Comforter, which is the Holy Ghost," Jesus promised the
faithful, "shall teach you all things, and bring all things
to your remembrance" (John 14.26). The Comforter is
"the Spirit of truth; whom the world cannot receive, because it seeth him not, neither knoweth him: . . . he dwelleth with you, and shall be in you" (John 14.17). Paradoxically, this indwelling spirit is also the descending
spirit which on Pentecost bestowed upon the disciples the
gift of tongues. Its traditional iconographic symbol is the
dove descending from heaven to Noah, to Mary, to the
disciples, to the faithful. There is no definitive evidence
that Stevens was at all preoccupied with the Holy Ghost,
but it is interesting and probably not coincidental that
two of his symbols for that aspect of imagination which
is immanent in man, in the world, and in poetry—the

chapel of breath which replaced the church—are the ghost and the dove. Like most of his formulations, these are double: one facet a critique of the old forms, the other a construction of new ones.

Ghosts in Stevens' work are most often the lingering wisps of ideas which deserve, but refuse, to die and the hollow forms of men who cling to these ideas and hallucinate others. Hallucinations are ideas without basis in reality, and the Holy Ghost in its traditional form would surely be for Stevens merely a sacred hallucination. There is, however, a tantalizing hint of another meaning for "ghost" in Stevens' poetry. Arthur Mizener, in an engaging argument that criticism is, after all, the work of living, pondering, fallible humans in pursuit of evasive ideas, senses this implication in the phrase "ghostlier demarcations" (CP 130) from "The Idea of Order at Key West." "Wasn't 'ghost,' " he asks, "the Anglo-Saxon word for spirit or soul? Is that why we speak of the Holy Ghost and does Stevens mean that this is his holy ghost?"[25] Considering the same poem, Eugene Nassar remarks that for Stevens, "in the best light, man's 'ghost' is equated with the imaginative faculty within him, the faculty impelled by will and desire to seek out 'ghostlier demarcations, keener sounds' in the phenomenological world."[26] For Stevens, the ghost is sometimes the consecrating, teaching, comforting act of imagination: the spirit of the grandfather descending to impart his knowledge or "the ghostly celebrations . . . / The secretions of insight" (CP 492) which are the manifestations of imagination in this world.

[25] "Not in Cold Blood," *Kenyon Review*, 13 (Spring 1951), 223.

[26] *Anatomy of Figuration*, p. 31.

Stevens' approximations of the Holy Spirit are not grandiose and apocalyptic but familiar and tentative. It is not the Holy Spirit bringing the gift of tongues but a grandfather, a ghostlier father, bringing "a momentary end / To the complication" (CP 303). In "The Lack of Repose," as in "The Bed of Old John Zeller," he descends to comfort, with "a few sounds of meaning" (CP 303), the troubled mind of his grandson. Stevens is clear that this is not hallucination. It is rather the incorporation of a spirit which, as Jesus promised, "shall be in you": it is "as if one's grandfather lay / In one's heart" (CP 327). In "The Lack of Repose," the grandfather of Andrew Jackson Something may be "a ghost that inhabits a cloud," but he is also a part of the near and the clear:

> a ghost for Andrew, not lean, catarrhal
> And pallid. It is the grandfather he liked,
> With an understanding compounded by death.

He comes to teach, and his words are "the intense disclosures" (CP 303) that Stevens elsewhere signifies by phrases like "ghostlier demarcations, keener sounds." These are secular, momentary visitations, but they approximate in the only way possible to the twentieth-century mind the comfort, knowledge, and consolation brought by the dove to the disciples.

The dove in Stevens' poems is also a descending yet indwelling spirit, and in its imagistic use both Stevens' critique and his construction of the Holy Ghost are more definite. There is some indication in "Sonatina to Hans Christian," for instance, that Stevens regards the myth of the dove as a Christian equivalent to the story of the ugly duckling. If the impulse to believe in a trans-

formation from helpless alienation and inadequacy into
perfect beauty and grace makes us identify with the
duckling who became a swan, "What," Stevens asks,
"of the dove?" (CP 110). Its comfort, he implies, is false,
the illusion of ducklings that are not and never will be
swans. But Stevens' most direct attack on the myth of
the dove is "The Bird with the Coppery, Keen Claws"
(CP 82), a poem with all the bitterness of "Negation."
In an echo of the biblical "king of kings" or "lord of
lords," the bird is "parakeet of parakeets," or, as William
Van O'Connor suggests, Paraclete of Paracletes.[27] This is,
like Joyce's substitution of dogsbody for God's body or
Eccles Street for Ecclesia, a savage pun, and it has the
further advantage of replacing the natural dignity of the
dove with the artificial, diminutive frivolity of a bird
that is man's mimic, the mindless repeater of his fantasies.
The parakeet is the negation—both the denial and the
opposite—of the dove. He resides "above the forest of
the parakeets" and "moves not": he is not immanent in
the world, neither comforter, nor advocate, nor teacher.
With white lids masking blind eyes, he is neither seen
nor seeing. Most of the poem's vocabulary is ambiguous,
and, as Louis H. Leiter points out, "the images create a
pattern of opposition: life, growth, movement . . . are
consistently confronted with their opposites."[28] These
antagonistic forces paralyze each other, as the parakeet
itself is paralyzed in the abstraction of its "pure intellect"
and in the self-absorption of its preening and flaring. This
is the Paraclete reduced to the absurdity of a parakeet,

[27] *The Shaping Spirit: A Study of Wallace Stevens* (Chicago:
Henry Regnery, 1950), p. 133.
[28] "Sense in Nonsense: Wallace Stevens' 'The Bird with the
Coppery, Keen Claws,'" *College English*, 26 (April 1965), 553.

a parody of what for Stevens the dove really is: the ennobling imagination either descending to or indwelling in man, alive, responsive, and enraptured in its contemplation of the changing world.

The dove which descends to earth is the sudden, unexpected access of grace which in "Description without Place" transmutes summer into "the spirit's universe"; our sense of the world is the "column in the desert," and it is this column "on which the dove alights" (CP 343) to bring radiance to coherence. This transmutation is the core of the enigmatic poem "Thinking of a Relation between the Images of Metaphors." As behind "Ghosts as Cocoons" is the Parable of the Ten Virgins, behind this poem is the pattern of the descent of the Holy Ghost to dwell within man. For the poem's fisherman, the wood-doves along the Perkiomen are images related to the image of the Holy Ghost: in the fisherman's "one eye," or totality of perception, "the dove resembles the dove" (CP 356). Natural fact remains natural fact but also becomes divine metaphor, and for that reason, in his

> one eye the dove
> Might spring to sight and yet remain a dove.

> The fisherman might be the single man
> In whose breast, the dove, alighting, would grow still.
>
> (CP 357)

The dove which "alights" here and in "Description without Place" suggests the imagination which illuminates; though Stevens is vague as to its source, it may come from the cosmic imagination associated in "Auroras" with the divine fire. The fisherman resembles the poet as

apostle searching images in the stream which in Stevens'
late poetry "is being / . . . the flock-flecked river" (CP
444). For him, natural facts relate to divine forces with
the precision of the relation between images of metaphors. The dove which alights in his breast brings the
possibility of a final stasis, a supreme metaphor, an imaginative integration creating radiance, peace, and harmony.

The dove grown still in man is Stevens' "The Dove
in the Belly" which "builds his nest and coos" for "the
whole of appearance" (CP 366). The opposite of the
metallic, indifferent parakeet of parakeets, it is the brooder deep within, "a self," as Frank Doggett explains, "rapt
by the continual, manifest showing of things."[29] Like the
fisherman, it has faith in perception, believing in natural
fact, and radiance in imaginative vision, believing in divine force. For this self, even the pigeon, the dove's
secular, urban equivalent, becomes a sacred manifesta-
tion and emblem. In "Sunday Morning," closing a meditation on the divinity within, Stevens presents the "unsponsored, free" earthly self in an image of soaring yet
doomed flight, as

> in the isolation of the sky,
> At evening, casual flocks of pigeons make
> Ambiguous undulations as they sink,
> Downward to darkness, on extended wings.
>
> (CP 70)

The indwelling imagination, open to experience, vulnerable to death, is finally for Stevens the only comforter and
advocate. It gives us, as an equivalent for the gift of
tongues, the gift of poetry; through it we perceive the

---

[29] *Stevens' Poetry of Thought*, pp. 147-148.

only truth available to us; and, finally, as Christ promised for the Holy Ghost, it is and shall be with us, considering all things.

If, in Stevens' series of substitutions, God is the imagination and the Holy Ghost is the imagination inhering in man, Christ becomes imagination incarnate: the poet or hero. As the Holy Ghost is to each man, God is to Christ, for "the Father," as Christ explained, "dwelleth in me" (John 14.10). The difference is one of manner and degree. The Holy Ghost, or for Stevens the dove in man, is private and still, a brooder on appearances, but Christ, or the poet who incarnates imagination, is public and active, a force radically altering society. Stevens' hero is, therefore, not only the contemplative man "lounging by the sea, / Drowned in its washes, reading in the sound" (CP 387) but also the captain, the soldier, the "capable being" (CP 330). Where the Holy Ghost, moreover, is the particle of God in every man, Christ is the principle of God: the perfect man. Every man, in Stevens' transvaluation, has imagination, but the poet is of imagination all compact and he acts through imagination to change society: "he creates the world to which we turn incessantly and without knowing it and . . . he gives to life the supreme fictions without which we are unable to conceive of it" (NA 31). Stevens' concept of the hero is complex and various, but one important aspect of it is the relationship between his hero and the hero of the Christian religion.

Stevens accepts Christ, Merle E. Brown notes, "almost as a model."[30] This is true not only in the larger outlines —the sense, for instance, of the hero as an intermingling

[30] *Wallace Stevens: The Poem as Act* (Detroit: Wayne State Univ. Press, 1970), p. 162.

of "substance and non-substance" (CP 297)—but also in particular details. Stevens was familiar with the life of Jesus both through early religious background and through later study. Reading in 1909 a life of Jesus was, he confessed, "like suddenly remembering something long forgotten, or else like suddenly seeing something new and strange in what had always been in my mind." The life of Christ remained strange and alluring to him, and he made his poetic hero a Christlike figure—a savior or deliverer, an intercessor, a martyr—but he was concerned as early as 1909 that the hero be as pertinent to twentieth-century men as Christ to the Palestinians. Visiting St. John's Chapel in New York, he was dismayed to find only the cross to symbolize Christ's life:

> When you compare that *poverty* with the wealth of symbols, of remembrances, that were created and revered in times past, you appreciate the change that has come over the church. . . . One turns from this chapel to those built by men who felt the wonder of the life and death of Jesus—temples full of sacred images, full of the air of love and holiness— tabernacles hallowed by worship that sprang from the noble depths of men familiar with Gethsemane, familiar with Jerusalem.—I do not wonder that the church is so largely a relic. Its vitality depended on its association with Palestine.
>
> (LWS 140)

The symbols encircling Stevens' hero are the symbols that surrounded Christ made relevant to us. The chapel of breath, unlike St. John's Chapel, is full of symbols and remembrances, ones which spring from Hartford and World War II as well as from Gethsemane and Calvary. Stevens did not exalt "Gesu" (CP 180), a figure as irrelevant as Herr Gott, but instead transformed him. As he recast the hymnal and the book of proverbs, Stevens rewrote the life of Jesus, and in the incidents from that life both his critique of the old form and his construction of a new one become clear.

The nativity of Stevens' hero has the theoretical implications and symbolic resonance of Christ's nativity, but these are cleared of modern debasements, the "familiar things in a cheerful voice, / Like the night before Christmas and all the carols" (CP 185). The hero is, like Christ, a man yet more than a man. According to Stevens' belief that "the thing seen becomes the thing unseen. The opposite is, or seems to be, impossible" (OP 167), the direction of incarnation reverses: God, that is, does not become man, but man projects an ideal abstraction which might be called an aspect of God. The major man, therefore, is "son only of man and sun of men" (CP 185). He rises from what Stevens terms the "commonal" (CP 388) or "the common self, interior fons" (CP 301) as a purer essence, "an extension of man, the leaner being, in fiction, a possibly more than human human, a composite human" (LWS 434). His divinity is the divinity of the brute self, not of an ethereal God, but as man exalted he becomes, like Christ, "the highest man" (CP 280), man refined into the godlike. "Excluding by his largeness [our] defaults" (CP 299), he seems, Stevens explains,

> To stand taller than a person stands, has
> A wider brow, large and less human
> Eyes and bruted ears: the man-like body

> Of a primitive. He walks with a defter
> And lither stride. His arms are heavy
> And his breast is greatness.
>
> (CP 277)

The biblical resonance relates the hero to Christ but
promises miracles which will be ours, not God's, because the hero is made of ourselves. The miracle of his
incarnation, his nativity, is the miracle accomplished by
poetry: the incredible become credible, the invisible become visible, the ideal become real. The hero "came
from out of sleep" (CP 299), Stevens indicates, "swad-
dled in revery" (CP 388), and "he rose because men
wanted him to be" (CP 299). As if to verify the instincts
behind the myth of Christ, he comes at winter midnight
heralded by a star.

Because the hero, confected out of the commonal, is
a "collective being" (CP 299) born in the spirit of imagination, Stevens can give, strangely, a sort of recipe for
his incarnation. "Make him of mud," Stevens directs,

> Devise, devise, and make him of winter's
> Iciest core, a north star, central
> In our oblivion, of summer's
> Imagination, the golden rescue:
> The bread and wine of the mind.
>
> (CP 275)

Through the flesh and blood of the hero, as through
Christ's flesh and blood, we commune with what is real.
Like Christ, the hero assumes being in the death of the
year, for winter in Stevens' seasonal mythology stands,
as Frank Kermode notes, for "pure abstracted reality,

a bare icy outline purged clean of all the accretions brought by the human mind to make it possible for us to conceive of reality and live our lives."[31] The symbols which surround the hero indicate that he is not only "luminous flesh" but also "shapely fire" (CP 297), for they are Stevens' winter symbols—glass, air, cold,. and winter light—which indicate ideal or absolute spirit refined from physical presence. They are appropriate to the hero because, like Christ, he is not only a man among us but an ideal beyond us. He exists in the world, Robert Pack explains, "as a possibility or abstraction."[32] "The golden rescue" he effects is possible because he is the force which brings summer out of winter, which rescues us from winter death by resurrecting the year. He is, as Stevens notes elsewhere, "winter devising summer in its breast" (CP 186).

As imagination incarnate, the hero comes in darkness devising light. He arrives "at the end of night" (CP 296), for, like Christ, he is the light-bearer or, in Christian symbolism, the morning star. In several poems, the hero is, like Christ, heralded by a star, the "heavy-fruited star" (CP 186) or "crystal-pointed star of morning" (CP 296) which usually symbolizes for Stevens the ideal inherent in the real: "the ever-living and being, / The ever-breathing and moving, the constant fire" (CP 238). The star is a symbol apt for both Christ and the major man since it can be, as they are, both immortal and polar. The major man, as an idealization of man and the possibilities of man, is

---

[31] *Wallace Stevens*, p. 34.

[32] "The Abstracting Imagination of Wallace Stevens: Nothingness and the Hero," *Arizona Quarterly*, 11 (Autumn 1955), 203.

The body that could never be wounded,
The life that never would end, no matter
Who died, the being that was an abstraction,
A giant's heart in the veins, all courage.

                    (CP 289)

He is an expression of man as he may come to be, and
hence, like Christ's, his incarnation is continual in the
hearts of men. An abstraction constantly blooded by
fresh transfigurings of the imagination, he is the one immortal man among successive generations of men. Finally, like the north star which is part of his confecting,
the hero is pivotal, for being the ultimate poetic creation,
he is "of the pole of blue" (CP 297). In his ideality, he
becomes an extremity of imagination around which all
else revolves, and he is, like Christ, both a direction and
an exemplar for lesser men.

    The hero whose nativity shadows that of Christ brings
like Christ a supreme fiction or Logos to earth. Just as
Christ is attendant to God, the major man, Stevens explains, is "part of the entourage" of the supreme fiction
(LWS 485). The Logos, or divine wisdom manifest in the
creation, government, and redemption of the world, is
often identified with Christ, and Stevens identifies the
supreme fiction with the major man, the man who is, as
"Notes toward a Supreme Fiction" defines him,

                    an expedient,

    Logos and logic, crystal hypothesis,
    Incipit and a form to speak the word
    And every latent double in the word.

                    (CP 387)

As Riddel observes, the major man is "the flesh become word rather than word become flesh,"[33] but he shares with Christ a double function as the word: he is at once the truth and the expedient form to speak the truth, the word as end and the word as means. Both Christ and the hero can say, "I am the truth" (John 14.6, NA 63), and both are bearers of the truth to man.

The hero acts upon imaginative man as Christ upon the believer: he defines him, delivers him, and promises him fullest life; he is, like Christ, "an example, that ye should follow his steps" (I Peter 2.21); and he mediates for us a reality not ourselves. As through Christ men come to the Father, through the poet-hero men come to the imagination and there, in the poem or the imaginative activity native to the poem, they are saved.

In traditional symbolism, Christ comes to men who are asleep in mental and moral sloth and, like the cock, wakes them to eternal life and light. Stevens' hero, as might be expected, wakes men from deadened, dreamless sleep into mortal, transient, and shadowed light:

> let the poet on his balcony
> Speak and the sleepers in their sleep shall move,
> Waken, and watch the moonlight on their floors.
> (CP 144-145)

Similarly, the villagers who slept as "the capable man" of "Mrs. Alfred Uruguay" descended from the mountain of his vision quickened at his arrival so that "time swished on the village clocks and dreams were alive" (CP 249). To bring to life is, in Stevens' pun, to conceive or define. If the imagination is the creator, the poet, like Christ, is his

---

[33] *Clairvoyant Eye*, p. 174.

agent: he "take[s] the place / Of parents, lewdest of ancestors" and "we are conceived in [his] conceits." He conceives for us not only our diviner selves but "the diviner health / Disclosed in common forms" (CP 195), the health which is, in poems like "Parochial Theme," "Esthétique du Mal," and "St. Armorer's Church from the Outside," salvation.

As the poet wakes us from sleep, he liberates us from the evil which is for Stevens false, outmoded conceptions of life which imprison the sensibility. The hero, therefore, is

the deliverer

> Delivering the prisoner by his words,
> So that the skeleton in the moonlight sings,
> Sings of an heroic world beyond the cell.
>
> (CP 261)

The skeleton assumes flesh in the promise of the poet as savior, the promise of an heroic world beyond any old conceivings. The singing of the skeleton recalls the unheard harmonies which, the poet prophesies in "Sad Strains of a Gay Waltz," will bring about the heroic world. The singer's harmonies

> Will unite these figures of men and their shapes
> Will glisten again with motion, the music
> Will be motion and full of shadows.
>
> (CP 122)

This, the secular equivalent of heaven, is reached not by apocalypse but by the evolution embodied, as Christ embodied God's promise of redemption, in the hero: it is "the hero-land to which we go, / A little nearer by each multitude," a place and time in which both the self and the earth will be divine in "an inner miracle and sun-sacrament" (CP 262). As Christ promised that faith in God will bring heaven, Stevens' hero implies that commitment to the law that "poetry and apotheosis are one" will bring fullest life. "If I live according to this law," the Pastoral Nun declares,

> I live
> In an immense activity, in which
>
> Everything becomes morning, summer, the hero,
> The enraptured woman, the sequestered night,
> The man that suffered, lying there at ease.
>   (CP 378)

The heroic world actualizes all Stevens' symbols of imaginative bliss. It is the immense activity vibrant in it, the activity of the imagination, which Stevens' hero embodies and exemplifies.

The hero is not only the truth and the life but also the way. As the principle of the perfect imaginative life, his activity is, largely and appropriately, speaking and breathing. The thoughts that "fall from him / Like chantering from an abundant / Poet" are "begotten at clear sources, / Apparently in air" (CP 277). They stem from the action of breathing and all that it connotes for Stevens. The hero "breathe[s] in crystal-pointed change the whole / Experience of night" (CP 298), and where the hero is, "the air changes, creates and re-creates, like strength, / And to breathe is a fulfilling of desire" (CP 301). As the hero takes into himself, refines, and recreates the air, so men must take into themselves, refine, and recreate reality. The way is imagination which empowers us to define and conceive a reality not ourselves, to merge ourselves with it as through Christ men merge with God, and to create in the process the radiance that is full imaginative life.

"The Son of man," Jesus said, predicting his crucifixion and resurrection, "must suffer many things" (Luke 9.22), but what he suffered and suffered for, Stevens would argue, is no longer as relevant as what the hero, "son only of man," suffers. "Lunar Paraphrase" (CP 107) recreates Christ's crucifixion, moving it from the spring, season of vital integrations, to "the wearier end of November," season of feebleness and disintegration. Mary, mother of sorrows, becomes the moon, "mother of pathos and pity," watching over the corpse of a too, too human god, the body of Jesus which "hangs in a pallor, / Humanly near." The scene, washed in sentimentality, provokes no strong, spontaneous reaction and thus can also become, in "The Good Man Has No Shape" (CP 364), the kind of scene Twain's King and Duke might concoct. "The Good Man" sketches Christ's life, a life of poverty and devotion to God rewarded in miraculous powers and ended by man's perversity. Jesus resurrected Lazarus, in Stevens' rewriting,

And Lazarus betrayed him to the rest,

Who killed him, sticking feathers in his flesh
To mock him. They placed with him in his grave

Sour wine to warn him, an empty book to read.

Jesus' death is as cruel, farcical, and meaningless as death by tar and feathers, and to add to the indignity, the feathers, which are, as Baird points out, mock thorns,[34] may also be mock angel wings or phoenix wings to accentuate the fact that there will be no resurrection. The wine, Christ's blood, has turned sour, and the book is empty.

The crucifixion translated into the twentieth-century context of Stevens' hero becomes as simple, striking, and meaningful as Stevens' substitution for the cross in "The Man with the Blue Guitar." Evolving man from Olympia into "Oxidia, banal suburb" (CP 182), Stevens thinks first of "an ancestor who is abstract" (LWS 791) and then sees him suddenly as an "old fantoche" with "his eye / A-cock at the cross-piece on a pole" (CP 181). This is the old abstract man, Christ the cock, "suddenly and at last, actually and presently . . . an employe [sic] of the Oxidia Electric Light & Power Company" (LWS 791). Revivified like the Pequod's mast covered with St. Elmo's fire, the cross has become an emblem in the landscape bringing, as the Company to the home, energy, light, and power to the mind. The old fantoche who hangs on the cross-piece is vague here, but he resembles the "central man" of "Asides on the Oboe" who suffers with and for us. "There was nothing," Stevens emphasizes, "he did not suffer, no; nor we" (CP 251). He becomes, more particularly, the soldier of "Esthétique du Mal" who discovers that "his wound is good because life was. / No part of him was ever part of death" (CP 319). The soldier, as Riddel demonstrates, is "a surrogate and secularized Christ, the martyr to man's fate and scapegoat for his imperfections."[35] In the sympathy that makes all men brothers and the hero not our father but our "bare

---

[34] *The Dome and the Rock*, p. 6.
[35] "The Metaphysical Changes," p. 72.

brother, megalfrere" (CP 300), in the unity, that is, which ties us to those we love, the soldier is soothed by life itself as, simply and without Mary's pathos and pity, "a woman smoothes her forehead with her hand / And the soldier of time lies calm beneath that stroke" (CP 319).

"The Men That are Falling," a poem written for the Spanish Republicans (LWS 798), is Stevens' pact with "lost remembrances" and his resolution of Christ and the soldier. In the poem, a man wakes in his "catastrophic room" (CP 187) to lean as if in prayer on his bed. He finds on his pillow something "more than sudarium . . . // The head of one of the men that are falling," a head that testifies to "the immaculate syllables" of its death (CP 188). In his acute reading of the poem, Ralph J. Mills observes that this "tortured visage . . . at once represents Christ and all other martyrs to an ideal cause."[36] His suffering and sacrifice, however, are for "life itself," not for glorification in another world: he "loved earth, not heaven, enough to die" (CP 188). The agony and triumph of his death are man's, not God's, and the poem rejects Christ's divinity, but there is in it, as Mills emphasizes, homage to the crucifixion as "a pinnacle of heroic tragedy that still belongs to the ordonnance of human imagination."[37] Here as in "Sunday Morning," however, our blood does not have to commingle with heaven to reach this pinnacle, for men in and of themselves can be divine and their sacrifices can, though bloody and final, redeem the time.

The death of a soldier is all the more poignant because

[36] "The Image of the Rock," rpt. in *Critical Essays*, ed. Borroff, p. 99.

[37] "The Image of the Rock," rpt. in *Critical Essays*, ed. Borroff, p. 99.

He does not become a three-days personage,
Imposing his separation,
Calling for pomp.
                    (CP 97)

The ceremonious resurrection of Christ seemed as hollow
to Stevens as the "Cortège for Rosenbloom." Doggett
suggests that Rosenbloom may be the Christian rose-in-
bloom and the poem Stevens' "version of [Thomas
Hardy's poem] 'God's Funeral,' "[38] but it seems more
likely that Stevens intended a wry and realistic rewriting
of the ascension of Christ. "From time immemorial the
philosophers and other scene painters have daubed the
sky with dazzle paint," Stevens explained, "but it all
comes down to the proverbial six feet of earth in the end."
To those who insist otherwise, he asked, "Why not fill
the sky with scaffolds and stairs, and go about like genu-
ine realists?" (LWS 223). Rosenbloom's fastidious carriers
bear his body to "the sullen hill," resembling Calvary, and
then up "the wooden ascents / Of the ascending of the
dead" into "a region of frost." The parade moves "to a
jangle of doom / And a jumble of words," a hocus-pocus
accented by the thump of the repeated end-rhymes
"tread" and "dead." Rosenbloom, "the wizened one / Of
the color of horn" (CP 80), is dead, body and soul, and no
amount of ceremony can resurrect him.

"There is nothing," Stevens pronounced, "more inane
than an Easter carol. It is a religious perversion of the
activity of Spring in our blood" (LWS 193). Easter
marked for him an earthly and imaginative, not a pious
and imagined, resurrection. It is, he wrote, "the most

[38] *Stevens' Poetry of Thought*, p. 126.

sparkling of all fêtes since it brings back not only the
sun but all the works of the sun, including those works
of the spirit that are specifically what might be called
Spring-works: the renewed force of the desire to live"
(LWS 879). Resurrection is for Stevens the cyclical re-
newal of life he celebrated in a poem placed "on an early
Sunday in April" (CP 254). The melted snow has left
"the gray grass like a pallet, closely pressed," suggesting
a grave from which nature has stirred. The ice locked
over the lake has cracked, and the winter stultification of
the man who walks around the lake has slipped into
curiosity and wonder. With the natural resurrection of
the year will come the spiritual resurrection of man, for
if the wind would blow and the water lash about, then

> the abstraction would
> Be broken and winter would be broken and done,
> And being would be being himself again,
> Being, becoming seeing and feeling and self,
> Black water breaking into reality.
>   (CP 255)

The black water breaking into reality, death rising into
life, resurrects the imagination of the beholder into being:
into seeing and feeling and the full realization of self.

"One's cry of O Jerusalem," Stevens wrote, "becomes
little by little a cry to something a little nearer and nearer
until at last one cries out to a living name, a living place,
a living thing, and in crying out confesses openly all the
bitter secretions of experience" (OP 260). Stevens' mystical theology is an exaltation of the near and the clear, and
his trinity is the cry to God made a cry to a living name,
our own, and a living place, our world. This cry triumphs

over the bitterness of man's mortality with faith in "the magnificent cause of being, / The imagination" (CP 25), with knowledge of the presence of imagination in every man, and with belief in the hero, the poet who incarnates imagination and through whose work we are saved.

4

HOW TO LIVE, WHAT TO DO

Why should she give her bounty to the dead?
What is divinity if it can come
Only in silent shadows and in dreams?
(CP 67)

STEVENS' mystical trinity is the center of his poetic faith.
From it, as from the central Christian assumptions, radiate
more immediate and humble inferences, statements which,
perhaps more acutely than larger, grander abstractions,
teach us how to live, what to do. Arnold's conviction that
"we have to turn to poetry to interpret life for us, to
console us, to sustain us"[1] is supported in Stevens' conviction that poetry must help us live our lives (NA 29).
Poetry interprets life by providing "the supreme fictions
without which we are unable to conceive of it" (NA 31);
by redefining values, it comforts "the heart's core against /
Its false disasters" (CP 372); in these offices and others, it
becomes for Stevens a sanction for life and an idea of
order to sustain us. Of all his poems in *Ideas of Order*,
Stevens preferred "How to Live. What to Do": "I like it
most," he explained to Ronald Lane Latimer, ". . . because it so definitely represents my way of thinking"
(LWS 293). With its blunt Anglo-Saxon title and ethical
concern, it is not the poem of a dandy, an ivory-tower
aesthete, or a confirmed hedonist. A moral and perhaps
even a homiletic poem, it is an informal exposition of a
scriptural moment, the expulsion of Adam and Eve from

---

[1] *Poetry and Criticism of Matthew Arnold*, ed. Culler, p. 306.

Paradise after the Fall. It introduces into Stevens' poetry the major symbol of the rock, and it is, as Ralph J. Mills indicates, "the first intimation we have of Stevens' idea of a *personal church*."[2]

Stevens' personal church, like his trinity, derives from elaborations on his statement that "God and the imagination are one" (LWS 701). If God is the imagination, biblical personae become aspects of our being, the various powers and abilities of the mind which in their sum constitute imagination (NA 61). In the coexistence and interaction of these powers, biblical history becomes personal history and each man may reenact the Fall, the access of grace, and the redemptive revelation. The sacraments, which are in Christian doctrine signs of spiritual reality and means to spiritual grace, become in Stevens' poetic doctrine symbols of the communion and marriage that come through imagination's grace. Finally, if God is imagination indwelling, sacred cosmology becomes secular psychology, and heaven, hell, and paradise become interior landscapes. This chapter, beginning with a brief examination of the symbol of the rock, will consider the structural details of Stevens' personal church, details which help us live our lives through defining a set of personae, a pattern of history, a sacramental system, and a poetic cosmology which, it was Stevens' hope, might make poetry as relevant to us as the Bible was to the Zellers.

In Stevens' "Two Versions of the Same Poem," old John Zeller, resurrected from his stout Lutheran world, confronts the alien turbulence of the twentieth century: the moiling of "that which cannot be fixed" (CP 353) in

[2] "The Image of the Rock," rpt. in *Critical Essays*, ed. Borroff, p. 97.

a terrifying "ocean of watery images," a thrashing of "elements, unreconciled / Because there is no golden solvent here" (CP 355). Between two worlds, Zeller is lost between two versions of the image of the rock, both of which solve or fix a world which, without a controlling image, dissolves into chaos. For Zeller, comfort came from Christianity, the church founded upon the rock and upon the Psalmist's faith that "the LORD is my rock, and my fortress, and my deliverer; my God, my strength, in whom I will trust" (Psalms 18.2). For his great-grandson, comfort came from poetry, the fusion of reality and imagination which creates "the rock of summer":

> the visible rock, the audible,
> The brilliant mercy of a sure repose,
> On this present ground, the vividest repose,
> Things certain sustaining us in certainty.
>
> (CP 375)

Stevens' appropriation of the biblical image of the rock was perhaps inevitable given his persistent adaptation of biblical forms, symbols, and vocabulary for secular and poetic purposes, yet it may seem paradoxical that the man who valued the image of the chapel of breath for its vibrance, radiance, and embodiment of the shifting relations between imagination and reality should also value the image of the rock for its solidity, its specificity as "the gray particular of man's life" (CP 528), and its fortress-like certainty of repose. The rock, however, is not a simple image, and Stevens struggled to show that if it is solid, it is not stolid, that if "it is a mountain half way green" to symbolize the empirically tangible, the definite, and the factual, it has another "immeasurable half, such rock / As placid air becomes" (CP 375) to symbolize the intangible, indefinite, mystical element man brings to the rock: the light of imagination. The rock's "basic slate" (CP 15) is the irreducible reality of the world, the real which is, Stevens emphasizes, "only the base. But it is the base" (OP 160). Above it lies the luminous air which, with the radiant ethereality of the chapel of breath, represents "the poem [that] makes meanings of the rock" (CP 527). These elements fuse into "a mountain luminous half way in bloom / And then half way in the extremest light" (CP 375): the rock of poetry, the church of the imagination. The image of the rock lies behind Stevens' use of biblical history, sacraments, and cosmology. It is, like the biblical rock, the truth and the object of worship and belief.

In Christian iconography, the rock represents the revealed truth of Christ promised by the church: it is "that spiritual Rock that . . . was Christ" (I Corinthians 10.4). Truth in the sense of a transcendent spiritual reality, the Christian Rock was for Stevens an imaginative construction subject, like every structure of ideas, to the erosions of time. Just as, in his effort to penetrate to fundamentals, Stevens reduced the cross of St. Armorer's Church to the sumac on the altar, the Light to the natural lights nourishing the tree, the Word to uncontained reverberations, spirit to breath, and salvation to health, so he shifted the meaning of the rock from divine force to natural fact. Stevens' rock, in one of its symbolic uses, represents truth not as transcendent spiritual reality but as the body of real things, events, and facts: actuality or, as he liked to say, "things as they are" (CP 165). In this sense, "the rock," unlike the Rock, "cannot be broken. It is the truth" (CP 375). Like the plum which survives its poems

(CP 41) and the wheel which survives our myths about it
(CP 222), the rock remains intact, a structure of things
unchanged by man's passing interpretations. It is the base
of all ideas, that to which man's imagination returns and
from which it speeds in "the swarm of thoughts, the
swarm of dreams" (CP 179) which constitute mental life.
It is in "Dry Loaf" the substratum of "sloping, moun-
tainous rocks" over which life courses as a "river that
batters its way over stones" (CP 199), "birds that came
like dirty water in waves / Flowing above the rocks,"
and soldiers, or all men in their combat with time, that
are "marching over the rocks" (CP 200) to the rolling
of drums.

The Old Testament songs of Moses, Hannah, and
David praise God as "the Rock of Israel" (II Samuel
23.3): He is stalwart, as "the Rock of . . . strength"
(Isaiah 17.10), steadfast, as the "rock in whom they
trusted" (Deuteronomy 32.37), and sheltering, as the
Psalmist's rock and fortress (Psalms 18.2). For Stevens,
these qualities must be attributed not to myth but to
actuality, for the rock of earth alone is strong, steadfast,
and sheltering. The Psalmist asks God to be "my strong
habitation, whereunto I may continually resort . . . my
rock" (Psalms 71.3), but Stevens asks only to live in
earth, where "the rock is the habitation of the whole, /
Its strength and measure" (CP 528). The rock is a measure because it fixes the stable bounds of our habitation
and because it endures, as a touchstone, beyond each
temporary evaluation of it. One of these evaluations is
the Christian Rock upon which the wise man of the New
Testament parable builds his house, counting on the
strength, steadfastness, and shelter of what could only
be for Stevens a local, temporary, and vulnerable myth.

In Christ's parable, "when the flood arose, the stream beat vehemently upon that house, and could not shake it" (Luke 6.48), but in Stevens' version, the house of God, like every other imaginative construction, cracked under the "ruinous storm" (CP 336) of change: "the wind beat in the roof and half the walls," and now "the ruin stood still in an external world" (CP 306). The wise man, for Stevens, builds on the bedrock of earth, the "rumbled rock" which underlies "the year's dim elongations" (OP 70) and which endures, strong, steadfast, and sheltering, beyond each temporary extension of it.

The rock as Stevens' familiar image for reality implies, as Frank Doggett observes, "that reality simply exists, simply is; it is there, it obtrudes, there it is."[3] In this sense, the rock represents things as they are, but things as they are sometimes for Stevens are things as they are upon the blue guitar, and the rock can also represent this. The truth of the mountain half way green is the enduring truth of the physical, the actual, the verifiable; the truth of the mountain's other immeasurable half of light and air is the temporal, momentary truth of the physical transformed by imagination and raised into poetry. This second half recalls the buildings of light and air Stevens called variously the "chastel de chasteté," the spirit's episcopate, and the chapel of breath, and it carries a similar meaning and symbolic resonance. Founded in the physical being of the earth as the chapel of breath is founded in man's physical being, the rock embodies the interchange of environment and self, visible and invisible, reality and imagination which is, for Stevens, the essence of poetry. As a whole, as the sum of its parts and yet

[3] *Stevens' Poetry of Thought*, p. 73.

more, the rock is "the starting point of the human and
the end" (CP 528) or, as "Notes toward a Supreme Fiction" explains, the "ever-early candor" of a stark perception of the real and "its late plural" in the imagination's
elaborations (CP 382). Like the chapel of breath, the
rock, in this sense, exists neither in the imagination nor
in the physical world but in the dynamic relationship
between the two. Like the chapel, the image can imply
change in the continuous circulation of air and shifting
patterns of light, yet the process it stands for remains
constant. The rock is changing yet abstract, vital yet
symbolic, and in this, like the chapel of breath, it is
finally "no sign of life but life, / Itself, the presence of
the intelligible / In that which is created as its symbol"
(CP 529).

It is significant that the symbol Stevens chose to represent the poetic process is the rock, for the rock is, as
Ralph J. Mills points out, "associated with the origins of
the Church in Christ's delegation of spiritual authority to
Peter; from this event there has developed an identifica-
tion of the rock symbol with the Church."[4] In Stevens'
poetry, the rock symbolizes a complex of beliefs and
values which present an interpretation of life to replace
those Christian formulations which, he feels, belong to
the past. For Stevens, as Riddel has noted, "the rock is
our worship, our belief."[5] The image underlies and illuminates many of his transvaluations, and its use justifies
Mills's belief that the "composite of sacred values har-
bored by the rock and held within the compass of the

[4] "The Image of the Rock," rpt. in *Critical Essays*, ed. Borroff,
p. 107.
[5] *Clairvoyant Eye*, p. 220.

mind" constitutes something that might be called Stevens' "personal church."[6]

Stevens' transvaluations of Christian forms, images, and ideas provided him with an emotionally and intellectually satisfying substitute for the exhausted religious systems of the past, but the formulation of emotional and intellectual order is not religion's only traditional solace. Christianity, like most religious systems, integrates ethical vision with psychological and cosmological assurances. It teaches men how to live and what to do. If Stevens' system was to be relevant to men who flounder in the chaos that baffled old John Zeller, it had to consider what would suffice in behavior as well as in belief. It had to confront the men and women of the time with patterns and principles of conduct which might guide as well as instruct. Despite his insistence that "the role of the poet is not to be found in morals" (NA 28) and despite his profession that imagination does not concern good and evil (NA 133), Stevens liked to think of the poet as a sort of secular priest.[7] He is "the appreciatory creator of values and beliefs" (LWS 526), and, in his highest form, he has "knowledge of good and evil" (LWS 370). His role

[6] "The Image of the Rock," rpt. in *Critical Essays*, ed. Borroff, p. 108.

[7] The poet "dwells apart in his imagination," Stevens wrote, ". . . as the priest dwells in his belief" (NA 66). He is "the priest of the invisible" (OP 169), the intermediary between men and a reality not themselves. Whitman's conviction that when the priest departs, the divine literatus comes, finds its counterpart in Stevens' development of an earthly leader who might be not only the extreme poet but also "the outer captain, the inner saint, / The pine, the pillar and the priest" (CP 185-186). When theology becomes poetry, the priest is replaced by the poet.

is not to be found in morals in the sense that he is not a moral policeman—"God forbid," Stevens shuddered, "that I should moralize" (LWS 195)—but it is "a role of the utmost seriousness. It is, for one thing, a spiritual role" (OP 206). Ethics need not offer a prescriptive code of behavior, for, in its most generous sense, as Stevens seemed to think of it, it is a descriptive theory of human values emerging in a pondering of the good and bad in human conduct. It is, like theology, the province of the poet.

Just as Stevens' theology draws from established Christian thought, so his ethics are founded in Christian forms. This is a result of Stevens' conservative habit of mind, but it is also a consequence of practical considerations. A poetry which "should address itself to the same needs and aspirations, the same hopes and fears, to which the Bible addresses itself" might, Stevens reasoned, have a similarly profound impact, but the modern poet could never "invent an ancient world full of figures that had been known and become endeared to its readers for centuries" (NA 144). This handicap is serious but not insurmountable, for by drawing on the biblical world the poet can preserve traditional resonances while formulating modern feelings. This method has two benefits: using figures and forms that are immediately recognizable and emotionally impressive, the poet preserves for his new context old reverberations, yet by implicitly contrasting sacred conclusions with his secular formulations, he proves the first outdated and the second germane. Stevens draws on biblical personae, biblical history, Christian sacraments, and sacred cosmology to help him consider who we are, what we must do, how we can find joy, and where we might finally and fully live our lives.

Biblical personae become in Stevens' work not religious exemplars but poetic and psychological examples.
As the concept of God dictated Judeo-Christian ethics,
psychology tends to dictate modern ethics. Before we
know what to do, we must know who we are, and this
for Stevens has intimately to do with imagination. If in
Christian exegesis God is plentitude, containing within
Himself all that is actual and all that may be imagined, in
Stevens' system God is the indwelling and interacting
imagination, and its plentitude is not cosmic but psychological. "The best definition of true imagination," Stevens held, "is that it is the sum of our faculties" (NA 61):
it contains all that we have been, are, and may become.
This definition promised to be both a psychological explication and a poetic resource for Stevens. As a psychological theory, it is related to faculty psychology, which
divides the mind into its various powers and explains all
mental phenomena through their interaction. The theory
might have attracted Stevens because it offers a rationale
for his frequent poetic personification of the mind's
powers, in rest or in debate, and because it offers a way
to make the shadowy processes of the mind seem concrete, dramatic, intricate, and vivid. "There is," Stevens
felt, "a perfect rout of characters in every man—and
every man is like an actor's trunk, full of strange crea-
tures, new + old" (LWS 91). In the simultaneous presence of these "various faculties," of these powers and
potentialities, "there is as much delight . . . as a man and
a woman find in each other's company," and in their continuous interaction, the "cross-reflections, modifications,
counter-balances, complements, giving and taking are
illimitable" (LWS 368). If imagination is considered the

sum of the action, the various faculties become the actors, and often for Stevens these actors take the parts of biblical personae and the script of biblical incidents.

Biblical drama often describes the conflict of man and God, as in Jonah's struggle against God's commandments or Job's acceptance of God's trials. The drama in Stevens' poems is most frequently man's "combat with the sun" (CP 46), the conflict between imagination and reality. Biblical personae commonly enter this combat as types, psychological possibilities of action or reaction. In "Notes toward a Supreme Fiction," for instance, Adam and Eve represent respectively the rational and the narcissistic in man, tendencies which impose upon reality an order alien to it and which thereby thwart the clear perception of it (CP 383). Their Fall, as will be seen, is not through willful misunderstanding of God but rather through inevitable misconception of earth. In the same way, Satan, first damned by his proud denial of God, becomes in "Esthétique du Mal" the type of the man whose "mortal no" (CP 320) denies the potentialities of earth. He is Stevens' "anti-master-man, floribund ascetic" (CP 241) whose obstinate negations project him from "one void into / Another" (CP 242). Like Mrs. Alfred Uruguay's, his "no and no made yes impossible" (CP 249). He is the cynic roaming outside the palace of the babies, like Milton's Satan circling paradise, while "in his heart his disbelief lay cold" and in his

> dark mind
> The clambering wings of birds of black revolved,
> Making harsh torment of the solitude.
>
> (CP 77)

The birds of black revolve in the mind of the cynic much as the priestly gramophones revolve in the mind of the mechanical optimist: endlessly, repetitively, fatally. The life of the self is for Stevens life manifest in change, and the rigidity of the mindless cynic, like that of the mindless believer, denies change. The negative is an essential pole; we must pass through it again and again to reach and affirm the positive. The damnation of Satan lies in the finality of his denials, in the obstinacy which closes his mind, hardens his heart, and ultimately imprisons him in a torment of helpless, unending, and solitary negation.

The anti-type of Satan is, of course, Christ, the poet-hero of Stevens' transvaluations who, like "the well dressed man with a beard," knows that "after the final no there comes a yes / And on that yes the future world depends" (CP 247). The Satanic no and no finds its answer

> In the yes of the realist spoken because he must
> Say yes, spoken because under every no
> Lay a passion for yes that had never been broken.
>
> (CP 320)

Faith in the possibilities of reality is rewarded in Stevens' system as faith in God is rewarded in the Bible. Acceptance of earth brings deliverance as miraculous as "the leaf the bird brings back to the boat" (CP 217); in "The Men That are Falling," it brings the vision "more than sudarium" of the man who "loved earth, not heaven, enough to die" (CP 188); and in "Cy Est Pourtraicte," it dignifies Ste. Ursula's offering of radishes, an offering which, like the herbs and apples of Emerson's "Days,"[8] testifies to the humble sufficiency of the earthly garden.

The poem "Cy Est Pourtraicte, Madame Ste Ursule, et Les Unze Mille Vierges" is partly a sly and suggestive joke, for it surprises God quivering with desire for his virgin saint. Stevens' irreverence, however, is for the God of the repressed Puritans and not for Ursula or the figure of the Virgin, a form of Stevens' symbolic woman. The symbolic woman is, as Doggett observes, the most recurrent and perhaps the most significant of Stevens' archetypes.[9] Naked and usually nameless, she stands variously for inner and outer reality, for the projected image of the unconscious which Jung termed the anima, or, as the embodiment of an attitude toward experience, for the poet's muse.[10] In several of these forms, she becomes the type of the Virgin: the intercessor, wife to earthly man as well as heavenly spirit, mother of God, and figure of an apotheosis recalling the Assumption of the Virgin Mary. As such, she provides a good example of Stevens' poetic rather than psychological use of biblical personae.

The One of Fictive Music is Stevens' muse of the imagination, the intercessor between man and the imagination as the Virgin is the intercessor between man and God. She is not a faculty of the mind but the mind's symbolic projection: a poetic creation of the same mythic proportions as the figure of the Virgin in Christian hagiography. It is, therefore, entirely appropriate that she is addressed in the rhythms of the litany as our

---

[8] *Selections from Ralph Waldo Emerson*, ed. Whicher, p. 451.

[9] *Stevens' Poetry of Thought*, p. 38.

[10] For a full and excellent treatment of this figure, see Frank Doggett's "Variations on a Nude," Chapter Three of *Stevens' Poetry of Thought*, pp. 34-54.

Sister and mother and diviner love,
And of the sisterhood of the living dead
Most near, most clear, and of the clearest bloom,
And of the fragrant mothers the most dear
And queen.
(CP 87)

In her "heavenly pity" (CP 88), she brings perfection "out of our imperfections wrought" (CP 87), the poem or the incarnation of the poem in imagination, and therefore, as the Christian in his loss prays to the Virgin, so we in our loss supplicate her to "give back to us what once you gave: / The imagination that we spurned and crave" (CP 88).

In a related symbolic projection, the woman married both to reality and to imagination as Mary was wedded both to Joseph and to the dove, becomes the mother of God, the origin or source of imaginative creation. The woman of "Sunday Morning," engaged in reality's complacencies as well as imagination's cravings, Susanna in "Peter Quince at the Clavier," for whom "the touch of springs" is at once "the green water, clear and warm" and "concealed imaginings" (CP 90), and Nanzia Nunzio,[11] whose "burning body" (CP 395) is forever covered with fictive weavings (CP 396)—each of these women partakes of Mary's dual nature. They are, as William Burney suggests of Susanna and other young women in Stevens' early poetry, "versions of the Virgin, giving birth, in

[11] Nanzia Nunzio, George McFadden argues, is a name which is "obviously cognate to 'Annunziazione' " and which, therefore, "links her with the figure of the Virgin Mary, as did the earlier reference to the 'immaculate beginning' " ("Poet, Nature, and Society in Wallace Stevens," *MLQ*, 23 [September 1962], 267).

transcendent purity of instinct, to the 'giant of the weather,' " to imaginative conceptions which must take the place of God.[12] As the Virgin was rewarded in her reception into heaven, so these women are promised a fulfilling, if strictly secular and limited, triumph over death. The woman in "Sunday Morning" is assured "the heavenly fellowship / Of men that perish and of summer morn" (CP 70), while Susanna is granted "immortality" in a "constant sacrament of praise" (CP 92) and Nanzia Nunzio, like the Virgin, espouses "an inflexible / Order" of redemptive illusion, the consoling, perfecting fiction which "weaves always glistening from the heart and mind" (CP 396).

Nanzia Nunzio's name comes from the Italian *nuncio*, which means messenger. Pausing before Ozymandias, a symbol of the conceiving heart and mind, she sparks the poetic moment; her visitation brings forth a redeeming illusion, what Stevens in explaining this poem termed "fiction as an extension of reality, or even as a thing itself in which we must believe" (LWS 431). This section of "Notes toward a Supreme Fiction" has a pattern which also inheres in "Le Monocle de Mon Oncle," "The Greenest Continent," and "Angel Surrounded by Paysans": the sudden appearance of an angelic figure who causes us to redefine things of this world. The pattern consciously juxtaposes the old and the new supreme fictions, for Stevens' angel is not a messenger from God but a herald of earth and his mission is not to convey God's word but rather to reveal "in the world about us things that solace us quite as fully as any heavenly visitation could" (LWS 661).

[12] *Wallace Stevens* (New York: Twayne Publishers, 1968), p. 40.

Angels which hover in heavenly visitation evoke Stevens' irony and pity. They are for him merely self-deceptions of the dissatisfied. They come to distract us from reality, and they represent illusion as escapism. They are, in a pejorative sense, angels of imagination, airy, ineffectual angels concocted by "sad men" to obscure the earth and clutter the sky (CP 136-138). Stevens' angels, on the other hand, are angels of reality, and the "reality" they represent has the doubleness of the "truth" figured by the rock: they may stand, like Nanzia Nunzio, for the seductive presence of earth itself or, like "the angel of reality" (CP 496) in "Angel Surrounded by Paysans," they may symbolize the higher reality of our imaginative transformations of this world. As an example of Stevens' use of biblical personae, the angel joins the psychological and the poetic, for like Adam he is one of us, yet he is also, like the One of Fictive Music, a symbol of the transcending processes of the imagination.

Stevens' correspondence details the inception and development of the poem "Angel Surrounded by Paysans," the most compact and the most important of his poems on angels. Letters to Paule Vidal, who found him the painting that inspired the poem, and to Victor Hammer, who considered publishing an illustrated copy of it, offer unusual insight into Stevens' intentions. The poem developed from a still life of terrines, glasses, and bottles which surround a Venetian glass bowl that contains a little spray of leaves (LWS 650). That this should have become for Stevens a group of peasants beholding an angel evinces not only the charm of his imagination but also the force of biblical language and lineage which made the terrines suggest mortal men "formed out of

. . . clay" (Job 33.6) and the fine Venetian glass imply the cleared perception of angelic knowledge (I Corinthians 13.12). The light penetrating the glass, the light of imagination which "fosters seraphim and is to them / Coiffeur of haloes" (CP 137), conspires with the leaves, which may have suggested here, as they had in "The Blue Buildings in the Summer Air," Noah's deliverance, to reinforce the translation of Venetian glass into necessary angel. The poem takes the dramatic form of a biblical episode, for, like the angel of Revelation who proclaims, "Behold, I stand at the door, and knock" (3.20), Stevens' angel is "seen for a moment standing in the door" (CP 496) in a place "in which a group of poor people were at ease on earth" (LWS 656).

Stevens intended the angel to be both a power of the mind and a symbolic product of that power, and the poem, therefore, carefully balances the psychological and the poetic functions of the image. The angel is "an earthly figure, not a heavenly figure" (LWS 661). As Adam represents man's rational knowledge, so the angel represents man's imaginative knowledge. "I am one of you," he declares, "and being one of you / Is being and knowing what I am and know" (CP 496). This is possible because, though an angel is above the level of nature, men, through imagination, "can / Do all that angels can" (CP 405). Like the biblical angels, Stevens' angel represents man's power and intelligence, his goodness and innocence, heightened into transcendence of mortal limits. His "simplest personification" might therefore be, as Stevens suggested to Victor Hammer, "the good man" (LWS 656).

Portraying the angel as the good man, however, would not only "make a very uninteresting picture"

(LWS 656), as Stevens admitted; it would also falsify the poem. If the angel is one of us, he is at the same time "the necessary angel of earth" (CP 496), an ethereal apparition in whose presence we "see the earth again, / Cleared of its stiff and stubborn, man-locked set" (CP 496-497). He is "only half of a figure of a sort, / A figure half seen" (CP 497), and he might, therefore, as Stevens suggested to Hammer, be left "invisible, as a mere influence" (LWS 656). As the good man, a psychological type, the angel is visible and concrete, but as "a man / Of the mind" (CP 497), a poetic creation, he is invisible and abstract, standing, like the angel of "Notes toward a Supreme Fiction," for "the fiction of an absolute" (CP 404)—an illusion, since for Stevens all absolutes are illusion, but nevertheless a consoling, perfecting illusion, a fiction in which we can, if only for a moment, believe, and a fiction through which we again touch earth.

The angel of imaginative knowledge is therefore for Stevens "the angel of reality" (LWS 753): he brings contact with the actual of the earth and he represents "the imagination, the one reality / In this imagined world" (CP 25). The "reality" figured by the angel, like the "truth" figured by the rock, is both spiritual and factual. These images form part of Stevens' exploration of the questions how to live and what to do, for they indicate the givens of human existence. Through biblical personae, as facets of the imagination in its interaction with reality, Stevens explores the psychological background of ethics in an effort to answer the question of who we are. Through biblical history, as an exploration of the cross-reflections and counterbalances of these faculties, he explores the behavioral background of ethics in an effort to answer the question of how we live. Stevens' mystical theology, a transvaluation of biblical events related to the three persons of the Trinity, is complemented by his ethical explorations, a consideration of the biblical events related to Everyman: the Fall, grace, and revelation. These events compose a pattern of life that is, in Stevens' terms, not imposed, or extrinsic, but discovered, or intrinsic. If ethics was for him a descriptive theory of human values emerging in a pondering of the good and bad in human behavior, it had to consider man's inevitable alienation from earth and the possibility of redemption through the reconciling imagination.

The problem of disobedience in the Fall interested Stevens, and many theorists before him, far less than the problem of knowledge. The sole reference to sin in his poetry is predictably to "politic man" who in the 1930's "ordained / Imagination as the fateful sin" (CP 143). The concept of original sin seemed to Stevens merely one of the nostalgias, a wistful, even sentimental, explanation of man's misery, confusion, and guilt. The consolation it affords is to Stevens meager and problematic, for in the traditional explanation both man and earth are cursed in Adam's sin. For Stevens, it is more noble, if more difficult, to believe that earth is neutral and to recognize that man's hope of "reality explained" is merely

> the last nostalgia: that he
> Should understand. That he might suffer or that
> He might die was the innocence of living, if life
> Itself was innocent. To say that it was
> Disentangled him from sleek ensolacings.
>   (CP 322)

The sleek ensolacings of the myth of original sin deform
an earth in which innocence has never been lost, for if
Stevens hedges the question of innocence in this quotation from "Esthétique du Mal," in "The Auroras of
Autumn" he affirms "the idiom of an innocent earth"
against "the enigma of the guilty dream" (CP 419). To
believe that innocence exists frees both man and earth
from the illusory taint of guilt, and Stevens is certain
that, even in the frightening auroras of autumn,

it exists,
It exists, it is visible, it is, it is.

So, then, these lights are not a spell of light,
A saying out of a cloud, but innocence.
An innocence of the earth and no false sign

Or symbol of malice.
                (CP 418)

Innocence, or freedom from sin, is a term Stevens applies
deliberately and generally both to earth and to life on
earth. By it he means not only that earth does not par-
ticipate in our disasters—disasters that come "almost as
part of innocence, almost, / Almost as the tenderest and
the truest part" (CP 420)—but also that, freed from
the inheritance of man's first disobedience, our suffering
and our guilt must remain our own.

As innocence is the opposite of sin, ignorance is the
opposite of knowledge, and in Stevens' special sense of
the word, ignorance replaces innocence as a blessed
state. The villains of the early poems are "the sterile
rationalist" (OP 67), the conceited philosopher, and the

academician of fine ideas, men who pretend, like Satan boasting before Eve, to discern things in their causes and to trace the ways of the highest agents. This, as Riddel remarks of the guitarist's desire "to play man number one" (CP 166), is "a godlike though fatuous desire to know the ultimate, a divine rather than human knowledge."[13] Like Eve's presumption, the ambition of men like "the moralist hidalgo" of "A Thought Revolved" exacts its own withering punishment. The hidalgo is the excogitating rationalist, the opposite of the mindless sentimentalist of the poem's first section. As Eve's seducer was Satan, his "whore is Morning Star," the English equivalent for the Latin *Lucifer.* Knowledge teases the hidalgo, as it did Eve, with promises of power and divine insight, but as it "dropped upon his heart / Its pitting poison" (CP 186), it proved for him, as it did for Eve, merely a bitter torment.

Stevens' solution is not that we become mindless or torpid, ignorant in a derogatory sense, but that we use mind and energy to evade the prideful preconceptions of knowledge and to remain humble, receptive, and joyful, ignorant in Stevens' special honorific sense. The ignorant, like the humble, "are they that move about the world with the lure of the real in their hearts" (NA 99). Unlike the rationalists, they efface themselves before reality, plunge into the complexity of an exterior world, and relinquish the will to power over things. This is "the courage of the ignorant man" who lives in the faith that "easy passion and ever-ready love / Are of our earthy birth and here and now" (CP 395). Because he has this faith, Stevens surmises, "it may be that the

[13] *Clairvoyant Eye*, p. 139.

ignorant man, alone, / Has any chance to mate his life
with life" (CP 222), and, paradoxically, it may also be
that the ignorant man alone has any chance to know the
basis of life, the knowledge that Stevens calls the first
idea. To attain this knowledge, one must first abandon
the false knowledge figured by the rationalist and phi- ·
losopher and "become an ignorant man again," for only
in humility and receptivity can man attain a definite, if
not a final, knowledge "and see the sun again with an
ignorant eye / And see it clearly in the idea of it" (CP
380).

Nothing, for Stevens, is fixed, least of all the condi-
tions of ignorance and knowledge. Today's insight stif-
fens into tomorrow's cliché, a static structure of ideas
alien to the flowing structure of things. In poems like
"The Man on the Dump," Stevens is jaunty about the
way knowledge ultimately falsifies the world, but in the
poems concerning Adam and Eve the process attains a
tragic inevitability. The Fall, in Stevens' secularization,
is the isolation of man from nature in the birth of consciousness.[14] Consciousness of self and consciousness of
the world, Eve's narcissism and Adam's rationalism, are
for Stevens variations of the pathetic fallacy. They project human conceptions onto an alien, inviolable world,
making the air a mirror and earth "a very varnished
green" (CP 383). For Stevens, Adam's dream is emblem-
atic of this projection: he awoke to find it true only
because he so willed it. It was the first man,

> Adam of beau regard, from fat Elysia,
> Whose mind malformed this morning metaphor,

[14] *Clairvoyant Eye*, p. 68.

While all the leaves leaked gold. His mind made
    morning,
As he slept. He woke in a metaphor: this was
A metamorphosis of paradise,

Malformed, the world was paradise malformed.
                                    (CP 331-332)

Adam's beau regard can be called either metamorphosis
or malformation: by whatever name, it is falsification.
The leaves leaking gold in the flow of light are part of
the "myth before the myth began, / Venerable and articulate and complete" (CP 383). Man's perception, by
distancing him from this flow, exiles him from paradise.
We awake from thought to find ourselves in "a place /
That is not our own and, much more, not ourselves"
(CP 383): paradise malformed.

Paradise was our own and ourselves, in Stevens' version of the myth, when imagination fully met and fully
accounted for reality. In paradise malformed, imagination creates and then faces what the poem "Saint John
and the Back-Ache" calls "the dumbfoundering abyss /
Between us and the object, external cause." If knowledge
from the metaphoric tree created the abyss, perhaps, the
poem argues, "the little ignorance that is everything"
may create

The possible nest in the invisible tree,
Which in a composite season, now unknown,
Denied, dismissed, may hold a serpent, loud
In our captious hymns, erect and sinuous,
Whose venom and whose wisdom will be one.
                                    (CP 437)

The serpent tamed in our hymns is a final transvaluation of the biblical serpent which first appeared, unsubdued, in Stevens' journal. With some unoriginality and much melodrama, he fancied the serpent—"an image of vice"—"triumphing, horrible with power, gulping, glistening" (LWS 91). The traditional, almost offhand explanation of the serpent as vice seems irrelevant in Stevens' obvious fascination with its writhing, and, not surprisingly, when the image reappears it has shed its allegorical skin. The serpent of "The Auroras of Autumn" is not the figuration of vice but the essence of change, the radiant flux and flickering of light in the aurora borealis:

> This is form gulping after formlessness,
> Skin flashing to wished-for disappearances
> And the serpent body flashing without the skin.
>
> (CP 411)

"This changeable serpent," Helen Vendler writes, "lives in present participles, gulping, wriggling, flashing and emerging."[15] It is pure matter and energy—elusive, absolute, triumphant, and unconscious. The voracious serpent of time and change bears the sheer menacing power Stevens failed to give his image of vice. Where the latter is the tired threat of an outworn myth, the former is a subtle, elusive transvaluation of the serpent which tempts to the knowledge of good and evil. It is the force that by rejecting man leads him into self-consciousness and then tempts him into the malformations of metaphor. The serpent is not to be tamed by human myths: not an actor in man's cosmic drama, the serpent is "relentlessly in possession of happiness. / This is his poison: that we

[15] *On Extended Wings*, p. 250.

should disbelieve / Even that" (CP 411). His venom is
his isolation, for he is venerable and articulate and complete without man. When this knowledge, Stevens implies in "Saint John and the Back-Ache," becomes our
wisdom, we may diminish the abyss between ourselves
and the object and we may, perhaps, momentarily redeem the Fall.

Stevens' description of the Fall from ignorance into
knowledge provides the background for his ethical consideration of how to live, what to do. In Stevens' work,
as several critics have noted, the Fall is fortunate:[16] it
gives man not only the privilege of redeeming himself
but also the means of his redemption. As Riddel summarizes, "In Stevens' secularization of the Fall, the origin of consciousness was the birth of imagination; man
grown conscious of himself wills to name the world, to
possess it as it once possessed him. He wills the 'I am' of
poem one, and in willing it completes his fall into an
alien world. The paradox is this: without self-consciousness there is no poetry, no need for the fiction which
marries self with world. The fall . . . is fortunate."[17]
Man's way back into the world is not to destroy consciousness and relegate all metaphors to the dump but
through consciousness and metaphor to repair the es-
trangement these modes of thought first, inevitably,
caused. The poems "How to Live. What to Do" and
"On the Road Home" concern the moment between the
expulsion from paradise in the consciousness which alien-

[16] Fuchs, *The Comic Spirit of Wallace Stevens*, p. 172; Roy
Harvey Pearce, "Wallace Stevens: The Life of the Imagination,"
PMLA, 66 (September 1951), rpt. in *Critical Essays*, ed. Borroff,
p. 129; Riddel, *Clairvoyant Eye*, p. 68.
[17] *Clairvoyant Eye*, p. 171.

ates and the return home in the consciousness which redeems. In them Stevens' analysis shifts from descriptive
to prescriptive, from what we are to what we must become.

The man and his companion in "How to Live. What
to Do" hesitate between two worlds: a lost land, by implication warm, fertile, and ordered, and a cold, bare,
and chaotic land symbolized by the massive, tufted rock
where they rest. These figures, as Mills indicates, "more
than suggest Adam and Eve cast from the Garden of
Eden."[18] Typically for Stevens, the question how to
live, what to do, is a question not of material action but
of imaginative conception: it is a question of the value
given the rock. The rock itself, unlike the biblical paradise, is neutral:

> There was neither voice nor crested image,
> No chorister, nor priest. There was
> Only the great height of the rock
> And the two of them standing still to rest.
>
> (CP 126)

In this elemental confrontation, the rock is at first the
victim of the pathetic fallacy: to the two figures caught
in the enigma of the guilty dream it seems part of "a
world unpurged" (CP 125). Innocent of man's guilt,
however, the rock is not unpurged but purgatorial, for
its neutral ground becomes a sort of expiatory state
between death and new life. It is not an action but a misconception which is to be expiated, and this misconception is for Stevens epitomized in the faith which attrib-

[18] "The Image of the Rock," rpt. in *Critical Essays*, ed. Borroff,
p. 97.

utes greatness, sovereignty, and splendor to the abstract voice and its priests at the expense of a world in which "the wind fell . . . / In many majesties of sound" (CP 125). The rock's majesty, like that of the aurora borealis, is its impregnable, enduring isolation. To understand this is to exchange the frightened debasement of exile for sudden, exhilarating freedom. Perceiving "the cold wind and the sound / It made" as "heroic sound / Joyous and jubilant and sure" (CP 126), the two figures are on the road home.

Stevens' "On the Road Home" finds his two figures alone in a wood. Having rejected the absolute for the relative, they can now reenter the world and possess it, as Adam once did, by naming. The rationalism and narcissism which lost paradise dissolve in the knowledge that "there is no such thing as the truth" (CP 203). This knowledge is, paradoxically, the little ignorance that is everything, the humility through which the ignorant man mates his life with life. It is what Stevens elsewhere calls "the nicer knowledge of / Belief, that what it believes in is not true" (CP 332). If this is difficult and sad, it is nevertheless liberating: it creates the deference which, for a moment, allows imagination fully to meet and fully to account for reality. Knowing that "words are not forms of a single word" (CP 204), we know that our words, if evasions, nevertheless give the world the only meaning it possesses. Substituting receptivity for dogmatism and feeling for theorizing, Stevens' two figures learn to discover rather than impose. Freed from guilt and from fear of change, they see as the poet sees. At that moment, the world begins to expand with possibility:

It was at that time, that the silence was largest
And longest, the night was roundest,
The fragrance of the autumn warmest,
Closest and strongest.
                    (CP 204)

The superlatives of this passage mark the moment of ripeness threatened, like the fullness and fruition of Keats's "To Autumn," by inevitable diminishment. Its warmth, strength, and clarity, made intense by their very transience, restore the world lost to man through his rational malformations. The earthly paradise is, for Stevens, to be regained, if only for a moment, in "the fiction that results from feeling" (CP 406), the perception that is the poem.

The road home begins in preparation for what one critic calls "the salvation of receptivity,"[19] a redemptive process illustrated by the structure of the poem. "On the Road Home" presents a series of moments in which, when man opens his heart by denying absolutes, suddenly, fortuitously, nature requites him in vision, so that, for instance,

It was when I said,
"There is no such thing as the truth,"
That the grapes seemed fatter,
The fox ran out of his hole.
                    (CP 203)

Setting his two figures on their way, Stevens leaves them, for the prescriptive in his ethics is strictly limited not only by his aversion to moralizing but also, more im-

---

[19] Glauco Cambon, *The Inclusive Flame*, p. 94.

portantly, by his belief in a sort of secular grace: an unmerited assistance given man for his regeneration or
sanctification. Despair, disdain, and hardness of heart, in
Christian theology, prevent grace, for "God resisteth the
proud, and giveth grace to the humble" (I Peter 5.5),
and in Stevens' faith also it is the Satanic figures—the
anti-master-man, the rationalist, and the cynic—who are
denied the grace accorded the humble and receptive.
Stevens can admonish men to prepare their hearts for
grace, but he cannot advise further since by definition
grace cannot be won. It is, in his poetry, the sudden, fulfilling, unpredictable, and momentary integration of reality and imagination which may come either through
a quickening of reality or through a flaring of imagination, through "the grace // And free requiting of responsive fact" (CP 263) or through a kind of perception
which may itself seem an act of grace. In both, it brings
the moment which redeems the fall and transports man
home to paradise.

Divine assistance is to Stevens merely a myth, but unmerited, unsponsored, natural assistance is a fact which
delights him. The moments when the bluejay suddenly
swoops to earth and clouds burst with whiteness are
moments of sovereign luck, for they "occur as they occur" (CP 222). "The major miracles" are those that
"fall // As apples fall" (CP 262), of their own weight and
in their own unpredictable, impeccable fruition. God's
dispensation of grace marked in an early poem by

> sharp Japonica—
> The driving rain, the willows in the rain,
> The birds that wait out rain in willow leaves
>
> (OP 13)

becomes in the later poems reality's unconscious provi-
dence, the fortuitous blessing when "the sparrow requites one, without intent" (CP 233) and "gray grasses
rolling windily away" prove nature's "deft beneficence"
(CP 155). The moment seems a grace given rather than
a vision created because these "times of inherent excellence" are "not balances / That we achieve but balances
that happen" (CP 386). They are, however, balances,
and they partake equally of reality and imagination, the
perceived and the perceiver. The redeeming events nature produces imagination absorbs and transmutes into
"redeeming thought" (CP 257). In most of Stevens' moments of grace, reality's quickening stimulates imagination, but this process can be reversed so that imagination's flaring exalts reality. In "The Pastor Caballero,"
for example, thought's improvisations make of a hat a
halo. The most banal object can become the most blessed
when, suddenly, "the actual form" assumes "outwardly
this grace, / An image of the mind, an inward mate"
(CP 379). The image of the mind is the meeting place
of imagination and reality: there, in a process of thought
figured by poetry, imagination's conceivings become the
mate of reality's productions. The moment of highest
poetry, the moment in which reality and imagination
balance, is for Stevens the moment of grace. Because
poetry can in moments such as this repair the damage of
the fall and bridge the abyss between us and the object, it
is, as Stevens proclaims in the "Adagia," "a means of
redemption" (OP 160).

Since it occurs as it occurs, the moment of redeeming
grace is beyond the reach of ethics. Ignorance is its sufficient but not its necessary cause, and, therefore, receptivity can only prepare for what nature and imagina-

tion must accomplish. Revelation, as a final biblical event
Stevens explores in his effort to discover how men live,
is more amenable than grace to ethical pondering. Ap-
pearing in both his poetry and his prose, "revelation" is
a word Stevens obviously enjoyed using: it lends sacred
resonance to his secular poetics, it exalts the poet into a
sort of prophet for a world lacking imagination, and it
defies religious illusion by becoming, in his transvaluation, the communication not of divine but of natural or
poetic truth. Stevens uses the word in two senses, and
the transition from one to the other traces a development in his poetic and ethical thinking.

In one of its meanings, revelation is for Stevens an
aspect of grace: the "awakening" which occurs in "times
of inherent excellence" (CP 386). As the metaphor of
awakening implies, revelation in this sense is a sudden,
effortless expansion of consciousness in which, to paraphrase Addison, we but open our eyes and the scene en-
ters. The imagination, like Stevens' Crispin, remains es-
sentially passive before the displays of nature, and its
poetry, like Crispin's, tries to record the text rather than
the gloss. The "perception" of nature, in a parallel distinction, replaces the "conception of the mind," for this
view of revelation holds that "conceptions are artificial.
Perceptions are essential" (OP 164). The assumption behind this distinction is that man can see into the essence
of things without the distortions of the perceiving mind
—without, that is, the curse of the fall—and it inheres
mainly in the early poems, where Blanche McCarthy
was asked to "search / The glare of revelations going by"
(OP 10) and where Crispin, searching the sea, "beheld
and . . . was made new" (CP 30). The theory of percep-

tion behind such passages, however, might well have made Stevens hesitate. As other passages from his work acknowledge, it is epistemologically unsophisticated, suspiciously mystical, and rarely probable, if even possible: usually, for the poet as for the rest of us, "if the day writhes, it is not with revelations" (CP 429).

Revelation in a second and generally later sense for Stevens is defiantly artificial, a vision achieved rather than a grace received. It is, therefore, a result of how we live and what we do, and it complements the ethics of receptivity with an ethics of conception. Perception, as Stevens well knew, is inevitably conception: poetry is less likely to be a "revelation of the elements of appearance" (OP 177) than "a revelation in words by means of the words" (NA 33). While the first suggests an Addisonian theory, in which the mind passively receives its awakening, the second implies a Coleridgean theory, in which the mind, an esemplastic or shaping spirit, creates its awakening. The certainty that "in images we awake" (CP 463) informs the important theoretical poem "Description without Place," which holds that we do not see into reality but rather into our description of reality, reality transfused and transformed by imagination:

> Description is revelation. It is not
> The thing described, nor false facsimile.
>
> It is an artificial thing that exists,
> In its own seeming, plainly visible,
>
> Yet not too closely the double of our lives,
> Intenser than any actual life could be.
> (CP 344)

In description, sight becomes insight and actual life the intenser life of vision. As St. John beheld reality suffused with God, the poet beholds reality suffused with imagination, and his poems become a text to replace the Revelation of St. John,

> A text we should be born that we might read,
> More explicit than the experience of sun
>
> And moon, the book of reconciliation,
> Book of a concept only possible
>
> In description, canon central in itself,
> The thesis of the plentifullest John.
>
>   (CP 344-345)

Crispin's hope to transcribe the text without a gloss folds in the knowledge that every text is inevitably a book of conception, a canon central not only in its importance but also in its position midway between reality and imagination. Revelation as an aspect of grace requires the Wordsworthian passivity of a quiet eye and open heart, but revelation as description demands the active, shaping maker, the man who knows he must labor to create. Words of the world create and control the world in ways known to the man who contemplates the words of poetry as St. John contemplated the Word of God. The ethics of conception involves the discipline of meditation upon the reconciling imagination, and in this Stevens' poetics become part of his ethics. Revelation as description is available to the man who understands that "the theory of description matters most" (CP 345). To this man, each act in the world is potentially sacramental, a sign of spiritual reality and a means to spiritual grace, and each place emerging in his descriptions becomes potentially paradisiacal, a place where, for a moment, imagination meets and marries reality.

The Fall, grace, and revelation enter Stevens' secular system to describe a pattern intrinsic to human life and values: man's inevitable alienation from earth and his possible, if momentary, redemption through a poetic way of seeing. As biblical personae help us to discover who we are, these biblical events help us to understand how to live and what to do. Moments of grace and revelation are rare and consummate moments of joy, but after the knowledge of what is good must come the means to acquire and perpetuate the good, and this, also, is an ethical problem. "Happiness," as one of the "Adagia" states, "is an acquisition" (OP 157): it is a matter of extending the moments of brief, intense contact with transcendent reality throughout an otherwise flat and vacant existence. Christianity solved this problem through the institution of the sacraments. The sacraments are, like Stevens' chapel of breath, "an appearance made / For a sign of meaning in the meaningless" (CP 529): by using poetic methods for a divine end, they further evince the affinity of poetry and religion. The sacraments make of a physical fact a divine force, for when Christ says, blessing the bread, "Take, eat; this is my body" (Matthew 26.26), an ordinary object is transfigured into a symbol of spiritual reality. When he says, "This is my body, which is given for you; this do in remembrance of me" (Luke 22.19), an ordinary act is translated into a moment of grace recalled and recreated through formal, poetic ceremony. For Stevens, the moment of grace—"one of the major miracles, that fall // As apples fall"—is also "one of the sacraments between two breaths, / Magical only for the change they make." A secular and poetic sacrament is, as Stevens defines it, "an inner miracle" (CP 262): the changing of natural fact into divine force. Sometimes his sacraments are sacred syllables rising from sacked speech, transvaluations of the formal Christian sacraments; sometimes, like the sacraments of breathing and of praise, they are new poetic creations rising from the knowledge that "if nothing / Was divine then all things were, the world itself" (CP 242) and from the resultant conviction, like Crispin's, that all the world's mellow yet commonplace objects, like the peach and the melon, "should have a sacrament / And celebration" (CP 39).

The seven Roman Catholic sacraments are confirmation, penance, holy orders, baptism, extreme unction, communion, and matrimony. Although it could be argued that Stevens sanctifies baptism in his quirky yet significant naming and that the ending of "Peter Quince at the Clavier," as William Burney holds, suggests the sacrament of extreme unction,[20] the two sacraments clear and central in his poetry are communion and marriage. These may have been most to his purpose because they symbolize a joining and can thereby figure the way in which

> Two things of opposite natures seem to depend
> On one another, as a man depends
> On a woman, day on night, the imagined
>
> On the real.
>   (CP 392)

[20] *Wallace Stevens*, p. 38.

Communion and marriage, by a simple substitution of the earthly for the divine, indicate moments of grace when things of opposite natures balance: moments when the bread and wine of the earth sustain the imagination and moments when the mind of man marries the body of the world. They form part of Stevens' ethical explorations because in them we discover not only what joy is but how and when we may create or receive it.

Communion, as the sacrament in which the faithful partake of bread and wine in commemoration of Christ's death, makes the flesh and blood of the deity man's own. In the cynical and materialistic society of the poem "The American Sublime," a society in which charlatans rule "mickey mockers" (CP 130) and "the empty spirit" resides "in vacant space," how, Stevens asks, are men to commune with the ideal—

> What wine does one drink?
> What bread does one eat?
> (CP 131)

The poem "In a Bad Time" answers that without an ideal, in an age of unrelenting and unrepentant realism, the Christian's bread and wine become the prisoner's bread and water and the communicant becomes the beggar who

> gazes on calamity
> And thereafter . . . belongs to it, to bread
> Hard found, and water tasting of misery.
> (CP 426)

The old adage that what we eat is what we are has a strange and striking symbolic pertinence to Stevens, since for him leaden men can only consume "leaden loaves" (OP 95). In the fading of all but the most debased beliefs, the miraculous disappears from things of this world: the self seems to know nothing but its own greed, yet nothing seems to exist except the self. In "these days of disinheritance," the Christian communion becomes a solipsistic cannibalism, a "cuisine bourgeoise" (CP 227) in which "we feast on human heads" (CP 228): the bread we eat and the wine we drink becomes our own flesh and blood.

The self-feeding, self-destructive isolation of solipsism finds a cure in poetry. "The wonder and mystery of art, as indeed of religion in the last resort," Stevens maintained, "is the revelation of something 'wholly other' by which the inexpressible loneliness of thinking is broken and enriched" (OP 237). As the act of communion for the Christian pierces man's isolation by revealing the divine, the act of poetry for Stevens rescues man by revealing the earthly: the otherness of life itself and the otherness of the poet-hero, the incarnation of imagination as Christ is the incarnation of God. In the moments of grace and times of highest poetry, cynicism vanishes along with solipsism so that "the eye believes and its communion takes" (CP 253). When the spiritual is found in reality, the glory of God becomes the glory of earth and Stevens can say, with biblical certainty, "Feed my lambs (on the bread of living)" (OP 178). The bread of living is a sign of the sweetness and goodness of life, but it does not need allegorical resonance to exalt it. This bread, like the "wine . . . at a table in a wood," is "a thing final in itself and, therefore, good" (CP 405). Coming from outside man, it helps him believe in something other than the self and thereby liberates him from solipsism, yet it does not pass beyond what exists and thereby saves him from illusion.

If through the bread and wine of life we commune with the otherness of reality, through the poet-hero, who is "the bread and wine of the mind" (CP 275), we commune with the otherness of the imagination incarnate. The poet's lines effect a transubstantiation of their own, for through them, as "Notes toward a Supreme Fiction" concludes,

> How simply the fictive hero becomes the real;
> How gladly with proper words the soldier dies,
> If he must, or lives on the bread of faithful speech.
> (CP 408)

Poetry becomes the bread of our being, the means by which the ideal infuses the real. It gives the soldier, the man in combat with time, not only an identity but also a faith to sustain his life and justify his death. In these lines, as Riddel asks, "has not language become our host?"[21] The poet-hero's language is to the multitudes "their bread and their remembered wine" (CP 254). It is "flesh on the bones," and

>   the skeleton throwing
> His crust away eats of this meat, drinks
> Of this tabernacle, this communion.
> (CP 278)

Communion with the language of the hero, like communion with the flesh of Christ, brings the moment of grace and fulfillment, for as Christ gave his body that

[21] *Clairvoyant Eye*, p. 183.

men might live, so the poet-hero gives his language that men might believe. The act of communion in Stevens' work becomes a sacramental act of language: the poem which, giving the ideal substance in reality, reveals and redeems.

To the Christian, the sacrament of marriage, like the act of communion, signifies a merging of the divine and the human. As the partaking of bread and wine is sanctified by the Last Supper, earthly marriage is sanctified in the mystic marriages of Christian exegesis: the union of the soul with the kingdom of heaven, of the church with Christ, or of Christ with Lady Poverty. Each of these marriages is "a matching and mating of surprised accords, / A responding to a diviner opposite" (CP 468) which easily and naturally fits the oppositions of Stevens' "universal intercourse" (CP 177). By his familiar transvaluation from the divine to its earthly equivalent in the imagination, Stevens' "weddings of the soul" (CP 222) figure the merging of the imagined and the real, self and not-self, mind and world. These weddings are moments of grace in which the poem or the poetic insight, gathering "the disparate halves / Of things . . . waiting in a betrothal" (CP 464), suddenly and spontaneously accomplishes their marriage

to the sound

Of right joining, a music of ideas, the burning
And breeding and bearing birth of harmony,
The final relation, the marriage of the rest.
(CP 464-465)

The "mystic marriage" (CP 401) is a near obsession in Stevens' work. Repeated to the verge of tiresomeness, the theme remains fresh only in the ecstasy with which Stevens returns again and again to celebrate it in all its phases: espousal, betrothal, wedding, marriage, or mating. It occurs in the union of flesh and air (CP 83), of the world and its central poem (CP 441), of the actual form and the image in the mind (CP 379), the sun and the dove (CP 519), "this mangled, smutted semi-world hacked out // Of dirt" and the "bloomy-leafed" bride of love (CP 119), and each of these marriages of reality and imagination generates a moment of full earthly satisfaction. Reality and imagination, like man and wife, become one flesh. Here, the constant juggling and shifting of opposites in Stevens' work, the war between man and time, man and earth, man and the illusory, subsides, and in the peace of this mutual fulfillment earth becomes, for a moment as long as midsummer, Stevens' paradise: "Axis of everything, green's apogee // And happiest folk-land, mostly marriage-hymns" (CP 373).

The transfiguration of an ordinary object or event into the symbol of a transcending reality or a moment of grace does not need the Christian pattern for its accomplishment. In Stevens' work, the sacramental vision is always available to the man who feels strongly and sees clearly, without the evasions of cynicism or the bolsterings of illusion. Earth is enough. It is our heaven and hell, and it is also our paradise, the place in which we prepare and consummate "a constant sacrament of praise" (CP 92). The image of paradise can be considered a culmination of Stevens' transformations of religious words, forms, and symbols: it grows from his religious heritage, the lineage and language of the Zellers, yet it breaks from the creed of the now deaf-mute church by affirming life, doubt, and the imperfect self. Like the

deaf-mute church, the Christian "Terra Paradise," in
Stevens' view, excluded "life's season [and] death's element" (CP 263) and exalted "the non-physical people,
in paradise, / Itself non-physical" (CP 325). To turn
from the static perfection of that unchanging land to the
pulsing, enduring green of earth is, like turning from the
deaf-mute church to the chapel of breath, a movement
from created object to creating force, from a sign of life
to life itself. The exaltation of earth is earned through
the hard thought of Stevens' mystical theology, in which
the cry to God becomes a cry to the all-seeing, all-powerful, and all-loving imagination that resides in every
man and is incarnate in the poet. In this faith, biblical
personae, sacred history, and the Christian sacraments
become a part of the near and the clear and paradise becomes not a reminder of our offense to God nor a reward
for behavior which pleases God but our birthright, the
place of earthly moments of grace and revelation.
Heaven and hell in his poetry become peripheral, useful
only as emblems of a psychological disaffection with
earth. "The great poems of heaven and hell," Stevens observed, "have been written and the great poem of the
earth remains to be written" (NA 142). Stevens' poems
of paradise are efforts to write that great poem, that supreme fiction which might show earth, transfigured and
transfused by imagination, as the final and fully sufficient
paradise.

"There is," Stevens always emphasized, "no other
world" (LWS 360). The land we live in, however, is
neither wholly of the earth nor wholly of the mind but
an infinitely, intricately variable creation of the "identi-
ties / Between one's self and the weather" (CP 258). The
climates of this landscape are, for Stevens as for Baude-

laire, also the climates of man's consciousness, and throughout his work the seasons find their analogues in the psychological balance between mind and earth.[22] Another analogue for this balance is the Christian cosmology. Since "both heaven and hell / Are one, and here, O terra infidel" (CP 315), they become not actual worlds in which the dead continue to exist but psychological worlds in which the living continue to struggle. We are "men whose heaven is in themselves, // Or else whose hell" (CP 186). As heaven and hell were once defined by their relationship to God, in Stevens' system they are defined by their relationship to the imagination. If the ideal state—the moment of gracious balance between reality and imagination—is Stevens' paradise, an overbalance of reality becomes his hell and an overbalance of illusion his heaven.

As Stevens conceived them, the pressures of reality in the twentieth century are so great as to seem "beyond our power to tranquillize them in the mind, beyond our power to reduce them and metamorphose them" (NA 22). Lack of imaginative control over reality produces two immediate and opposite dangers: paralysis within the real or escape into illusion. The poet's "infernal walls" are the untranquillized actualities that clutter the landscape, "the cigar stores, / Ryan's lunch, hatters, insurance and medicines" (CP 185) which, if not abstracted and controlled by the imagination, overwhelm the mind. Hell for Stevens is the winter world in which, in the absence of imagination, reality starkly and bleakly triumphs over the mind. This world finds its definition

[22] For an excellent discussion of Stevens' poetic landscapes, see Richard A. Macksey, "The Climates of Wallace Stevens," *The Act of the Mind*, ed. Pearce and Miller, pp. 185-223.

only in negatives and in nothingness: it is the landscape of "No Possum, No Sop, No Taters." The sun is absent, the field frozen, the leaves dry, the sky hard. As both Frank Doggett[23] and Karl Wentersdorf[24] have observed, this is the landscape of Dante's *Inferno*: the broken, mutilated stalks which "have arms without hands . . . trunks / Without legs or, for that, without heads" (CP 293-294), the rusty crow with malicious eye rising like a bad angel into the air, the emptiness in which "bad is final" (CP 293), all these images evoke the memory of the ultimate evil and bitter cold at the bottom of hell. Like the mechanical hell in "A Thought Revolved," this is a netherworld of the living dead. The pain seems unbearable because the imagination, the force which might counter and conquer it, is absent. If hell is not exactly a place of punishment for Stevens, it is yet a place to be escaped through the resurrection of imagination. The redemptive fiction, in which we assume responsibility for pain as for pleasure and through which we know the health of the world to be enough, assimilates hell, so that in "Esthétique du Mal" Stevens' ethic of receptivity and his ethic of conception make it seem

> As if hell, so modified, had disappeared,
> As if pain, no longer satanic mimicry,
> Could be borne, as if we were sure to find our way.
>
> (CP 316)

Hell is not, as Sartre felt, other people: it is the paralysis

[23] "Wallace Stevens' Secrecy of Words: A Note on Import in Poetry," *New England Quarterly*, 31 (September 1958), 378-379.
[24] "Wallace Stevens, Dante Alighieri, and the Emperor," *Twentieth Century Literature*, 13 (January 1968), 198.

of our own imagination, and it can be harrowed by the regenerating illusion figured by the supreme fiction.

In considering the value of illusion, Stevens always distinguished between illusion which regenerates and illusion which enervates: the first enhances reality with the force of feeling, the second belittles it with the force of sentimentality. While the achievement of the one is the abstraction of the supreme fiction, the achievement of the other lies in what Stevens calls "minor wish-fulfillments" (NA 139). Heaven represents the second kind of illusion. Easy targets bored Stevens, and when he assaults "empty heaven and its hymns" (CP 167), the effect is often as flat as some of his attacks on the deaf-mute church. "Eventually," as one of the "Adagia" runs, "an imaginary world is entirely without interest" (OP 175), and heaven for Stevens epitomizes the imaginary. Dangerous only if it diverts attention from earth, heaven is a cliché land "full of Raphael's costumes" (OP 5), hung with "flash drapery" (CP 274), and peopled by "pearly women that drop / . . . and float in air" (CP 464). It sparked him only when it provided the opportunity for a wry wink, as in his equation of "the dream / Of heaven" with Marx's dream of the future (OP 65), or for a sly inversion, as in his definition of heaven as a tomb (CP 56). Finding a punishment to fit the crime fascinated Stevens as it did Dante, but Stevens' penalties are for the devotees of heaven. "What a ghastly situation it would be," he gleefully speculated, ". . . if as life ends, instead of passing to a former Victorian sphere, we passed into a land in which none of our problems had been solved, after all, and nothing resembled anything we have ever known" (NA 76-77). In this speculation, heaven becomes at best a sort of limbo and at worst hell itself, a land of

wandering ghosts "about and still about / To find whatever it is they seek" (CP 56). If Stevens' joke on Cotton
Mather was that the heaven he exalted proved merely
"the blank" (CP 217), from this blank the ghosts of
"Large Red Man Reading" return to hear the poet's
exaltation of earth. Like the dead of the *Odyssey* hunger-
ing for life,[25]

> They were those that would have wept to step
>   barefoot into reality,
>
> That would have wept and been happy, have
>   shivered in the frost
> And cried out to feel it again, have run fingers
>   over leaves
> And against the most coiled thorn, have seized
>   on what was ugly
>
> And laughed.
>   (CP 423-424)

In a cruelly fit and poignant turn, those who glorified
the ornate and ethereal become as thin and spent as their
dream. Yearning for the simplest, sharpest earthly things,
they discover what they should have known from the
beginning, that, as Stevens always stressed, "the indifferent experience of life is the unique experience, the
item of ecstasy which we have been isolating and re-
serving for another time and place, loftier and more se-
cluded" (OP 213).

[25] Doggett, "Wallace Stevens and the World We Know,"
English Journal, 48 (October 1959), 370.

What is man to gain, Stevens' poems ask, if in hope of a far-off, haunted land, he loses the whole world and, most certainly and devastatingly, forfeits his soul? The ghosts who long to step barefoot into reality are men whose blood has failed in the sad waste of the instinct for heaven. This instinct has its counterpart, however, in the earthly poems of the large red man, poems of "the pans above the stove, the pots on the table, the tulips among them" (CP 423). The instinct for earth demands the will to make our blood the blood of paradise and the knowledge that, freed from the nostalgias which endow a phantom land with the glory of earth, we do not lose the glory of heaven. The return to the pots, pans, and tulips of earth restores to what is close and real the radiance falsely attributed to transcendent realms, and it restores to the poet, or every man of imagination, the dignity, power, and responsibility falsely attributed to transcendent beings. Through Stevens' lineage and language, through the ethos of the chapel of breath and the carefully considered formulations of his mystical theology shines the certain faith that "the brilliance of earth is the brilliance of every paradise" (NA 77). Earth is all of paradise we shall know, and it holds every exaltation, every grace and revelation, available to man. This faith rarely wavers in Stevens' work, for from *Harmonium* to *The Rock* his poems of paradise insist that the central, luminous, warm, and fertile earth in which imagination meets and marries reality yields man's entire solace and his every sanction.

Poems like "Esthétique du Mal," "Description without Place," and "A Thought Revolved" prepare for Stevens' visions of paradise, in Riddel's phrase, as dogma prepares for ritual: "the one precedes the other not logically but as preparation for devotion precedes devotion proper."[26] Stevens' "Sunday Morning" service, consecrated to earth, dispels the hush of puritan Sundays with the boisterous, brilliant freedom of the sun which, in Stevens' transvaluations, is neither Christ nor the divine light but the "savage source" (CP 70) of life itself. The poet-priest conducts the service with a catechism and an incantation redefining the sacred as the responsive and the perceptive in human feeling: the passions, grievings, elations, and emotions which must now "be cherished like the thought of heaven" (CP 67). Man's pleasures and pains replace the monotonous perfection of heaven's "imperishable bliss" (CP 68) with an intensity won through their very impermanence. This is a paradise of the imperfect, composed of an immense beauty both compellingly possible and endlessly passing:

> Deer walk upon our mountains, and the quail
> Whistle about us their spontaneous cries;
> Sweet berries ripen in the wilderness;
> And, in the isolation of the sky,
> At evening, casual flocks of pigeons make
> Ambiguous undulations as they sink,
> Downward to darkness, on extended wings.
>
> (CP 70)

This earthly paradise is the imagination's gift, a grace which falls as the dew falls to refresh and irradiate the world. Through imagination, earth becomes, as no mythic land or aloof, ethereal heaven could, "a part of labor and a part of pain" (CP 68), as supple and as turbulent as

[26] *Clairvoyant Eye*, p. 216.

the men who, caught in its joys, chant the "chant of paradise, / Out of their blood" (CP 70).

In Stevens' dark period, which stretched from *Ideas of Order* through *Owl's Clover*, the summer weather of *Harmonium* shrank into an autumnal bleakness in which Stevens, like Adam and Eve of "How to Live. What to Do," confronted the cold wind and bare rock of a recalcitrant world. The saving rediscovery of "The Man with the Blue Guitar" is the grace of imagination, the moment of brilliant balance in which "the thinking of art seems final when // The thinking of god is smoky dew" (CP 168). The sensual and spontaneous integrations of "Sunday Morning" pass into a new, more intellectual belief centered in the imagination's activity and in the sober knowledge that "final belief / Must be in a fiction. It is time to choose" (CP 250). This affirmation came, for Stevens,

> in the imagination's new beginning,
> In the yes of the realist spoken because he must
> Say yes, spoken because under every no
> Lay a passion for yes that had never been broken.
> (CP 320)

In this acceptance of the redeeming fiction, the emotions of "Sunday Morning" become Stevens' riper, firmer "Credences of Summer."

"Credences of Summer" is Stevens' consummate hymn to the paradise of living, finally and fully, as and where we live. The subject is the moment of total satisfaction in which "the roses are heavy with a weight / Of fragrance and the mind lays by its trouble" (CP 372). It is "green's green apogee" (CP 373) when the conjunction of desire and object is fullest and when we are, for a moment, "complete in a completed scene" (CP 378). Without evasion by any metaphor, imagination suffuses reality in the "pure rhetoric of a language without words" (CP 374). Here, when, in Isabel G. MacCaffrey's terms, "reality fills, masters, and satisfies the mind,"[27] we "postpone the anatomy of summer" (CP 373), for this is the completeness that refuses even the contemplation of itself. We say only

> this, this is the centre that I seek.
> Fix it in an eternal foliage
>
> And fill the foliage with arrested peace,
> Joy of such permanence, right ignorance
> Of change still possible. Exile desire
> For what is not. This is the barrenness
> Of the fertile thing that can attain no more.
>   (CP 373)

The peace and joy of this moment are untouched by change still possible because this is the time of "right ignorance" which places man at the still point of a turning world: "the natural tower of all the world, / The point of survey . . . / Axis of everything" (CP 373). The mountain on which the tower rests is, as several critics have pointed out, the archetypal mountain of the earthly paradise, the *axis mundi* or place of epiphany midway between the mutable world of earth and the eternal world of the heavens.[28] It is also Stevens' rock at the

---

[27] "The Other Side of Silence: 'Credences of Summer' as an Example," *MLQ*, 30 (September 1969), 421.

[28] Harold Bloom, *The Visionary Company: A Reading of Eng-*

center of earth and the center of consciousness, the rock
of the church become the rock of poetry: "the visible
rock, the audible, / The brilliant mercy of a sure repose"
(CP 375). The mercy and the certainty of this rock is
the conjunction of imagination and reality in credence.

If "Credences" is Stevens' consummate hymn to summer, the power it addresses is the imagination whose
divine attributes allow man to recognize, instantly and
intuitively, that earth is the final abode of peace, harmony, and grace. "Notes toward a Supreme Fiction,"
dedicated to the imagination and the "vivid transparence" (CP 380) it creates, celebrates in what Wordsworth called "spousal verse" the marriage of the mind
and nature through the union of the great Captain and
the maiden Bawda. As Christians love one another "in
Christ," the Captain and the maiden love each other "in
Catawba,"[29] in earth itself:

> They married well because the marriage-place
> Was what they loved. It was neither heaven nor hell.
> They were love's characters come face to face.
>
> (CP 401)

This "mystic marriage," as Doggett observes, is an allegory of "the mind's share in creating reality."[30] The
great captain, like other of Stevens' soldiers and heroes,
represents the mind, "his high, / His puissant front" sig-
naling the force of his intellect and imagination. His love

---

lish Romantic Poetry (Garden City, N.Y.: Doubleday, 1961), p.
10; J. Dennis Huston, *"Credences of Summer*: An Analysis," *MP*,
67 (February 1970), 265.

[29] Vendler, *On Extended Wings*, p. 181.

[30] *Stevens' Poetry of Thought*, p. 103.

of the real is consummated in marriage only after he
foreswears the desire to probe earth's arcana, or, in
Stevens' pun, "the shoo-shoo-shoo of secret cymbals
round," and comes to accept instead the thing itself: "the
ever-hill Catawba," at once maiden and bawd. Incessantly married yet ever virginal, Bawda represents the
sensuous reality of earth, and she accepts her lover as
part of herself, for she "loved the captain as she loved
the sun." Their union creates Catawba, a word which
fuses their names to symbolize what Stevens called "these
// Elysia, these days, half earth, half mind; / Half sun,
half thinking of the sun" (CP 257). Their marriage is
another form of the *axis mundi* or central point of the
world, for it occurs "at noon . . . on the mid-day of the
year." The marriage service, conducted in Stevens' religious imagery, contains a "ceremonial hymn," the once
foresworn and now communal "sipping of the marriage
wine," and the revelation which becomes for Stevens
the essential poem at the center of things. It is a "sign /
To stop the whirlwind, balk the elements" (CP 401): the
brief, intense meeting that shatters nature to produce the
supreme fiction, the total integration of reality and imagination, earth and mind, visible and invisible. A momentary truce in the "war between the mind / And sky,
between thought and day and night" (CP 407), it brings
the vivid transparence of a peace that passes understanding.

When all things meet in "the huge, high harmony that
sounds / A little and a little, suddenly" (CP 440), the
landscape of the world becomes the landscape of paradise, part of the apotheosis that for Stevens is poetry. In
this moment, it is enough

To have satisfied the mind and turn to see,
(That being as much belief as we may have,)
And turn to look and say there is no more
Than this, in this alone I may believe,
Whatever it may be; then one's belief
Resists each past apocalypse.

(CP 257)

Stevens' belief persisted through the stark and frigid
visions of "The Auroras of Autumn" and the mellower
reconciliations of "The Rock" into the last of his collected poems. "Not Ideas about the Thing but the Thing
Itself" (CP 534) celebrates the meagerest of reality's be-
quests: "a bird's cry, at daylight or before, / In the early
March wind." The cry comes to him like a ghost hunger-
ing for life, and he, like the large red man, exalts it in a
vision of grace and revelation:

That scrawny cry—it was
A chorister whose c preceded the choir.
It was part of the colossal sun,

Surrounded by its choral rings,
Still far away. It was like
A new knowledge of reality.

Stevens, like his ancestors the Zellers, came to his knowledge of reality through a belief incorporating religious
symbol, form, and language. His fully found and fully
made substitute for religion, teaching him how to live
and what to do, formed of the world a place his own
and, much more, himself. For Stevens, our blood will not

fail. In the faith of the chapel of breath, in the hope which overcomes negations, and in the charity which is the imagination's love for the world, the earth, for Stevens, not only seems but actually and miraculously is all of paradise we shall know.

SELECTED BIBLIOGRAPHY

The following sources, a limited selection from the bulk of Stevens criticism, have proved useful in the study of Stevens' search for a poetic religion. Included here are all of the books on Stevens published through 1971, all of the articles cited within the text, and, as space allowed, other sources pertinent to the subject. I have not listed many of the helpful articles reprinted in the three readily available collections of essays on Stevens, nor was it possible to cite many other excellent essays on related aspects of Stevens' poetry and thought.

Primary Sources

Stevens, Wallace. *The Collected Poems of Wallace Stevens.* New York: Alfred A. Knopf, 1954.

———. *Letters of Wallace Stevens.* Selected and Edited by Holly Stevens. New York: Alfred A. Knopf, 1966.

———. *The Necessary Angel: Essays on Reality and the Imagination.* New York: Alfred A. Knopf, 1951.

———. *Opus Posthumous.* Ed., with an Introduction, by Samuel French Morse. New York: Alfred A. Knopf, 1957.

———. *The Palm at the End of the Mind: Selected Poems and a Play by Wallace Stevens.* Ed. Holly Stevens. New York: Alfred A. Knopf, 1971.

———. [Notes on the poems]. *Wallace Stevens: Mattino Domenicale ed Altre Poesie.* Trans. Renato Poggioli. Torino: Guilio Einuadi, 1954.

Secondary Sources

I. Book-Length Studies of Stevens

The Achievement of Wallace Stevens. Ed. Ashley Brown and Robert S. Haller. New York: J. B. Lippincott, 1962.

The Act of the Mind: Essays on the Poetry of Wallace Stevens. Ed. Roy Harvey Pearce and J. Hillis Miller. Baltimore: Johns Hopkins Press, 1965.

Baird, James. *The Dome and the Rock: Structure in the Poetry of Wallace Stevens.* Baltimore: Johns Hopkins Press, 1968.

Benamou, Michel. *Wallace Stevens and the Symbolist Imagination.* Princeton: Princeton Univ. Press, 1972.

Blessing, Richard Allen. *Wallace Stevens' "Whole Harmonium."* Syracuse: Syracuse Univ. Press, 1970.

Brown, Merle E. *Wallace Stevens: The Poem as Act.* Detroit: Wayne State Univ. Press, 1970.

Burney, William. *Wallace Stevens.* New York: Twayne Publishers, 1968.

Buttel, Robert. *Wallace Stevens: The Making of Harmonium.* Princeton: Princeton Univ. Press, 1967.

Doggett, Frank. *Stevens' Poetry of Thought.* Baltimore: Johns Hopkins Press, 1966.

Enck, John J. *Wallace Stevens: Images and Judgments.* Carbondale: Southern Illinois Univ. Press, 1964.

Fuchs, Daniel. *The Comic Spirit of Wallace Stevens.* Durham, N.C.: Duke Univ. Press, 1963.

Kermode, Frank. *Wallace Stevens.* New York: Grove Press, 1961.

Kessler, Edward. *Images of Wallace Stevens.* New Brunswick, N.J.: Rutgers Univ. Press, 1972.

Lentricchia, Frank. *The Gaiety of Language: An Essay on the Radical Poetics of W. B. Yeats and Wallace Stevens.* Berkeley: Univ. of California Press, 1968.

Morse, Samuel French, *Wallace Stevens: Poetry as Life.* New York: Pegasus, 1970

————. *Wallace Stevens: A Preliminary Checklist of His Published Writings, 1898-1954.* New Haven: Yale Univ. Library, 1954.

————, Jackson R. Bryer, and Joseph N. Riddel. *Wallace Stevens: Checklist and Bibliography of Stevens Criticism.* Denver: Alan Swallow, 1963.

Nassar, Eugene Paul. *Wallace Stevens: An Anatomy of Figuration.* Philadelphia: Univ. of Pennsylvania Press, 1965.

O'Connor, William Van. *The Shaping Spirit: A Study of Wallace Stevens.* Chicago: Henry Regnery, 1950.

Pack, Robert. *Wallace Stevens: An Approach to His Poetry and Thought.* New Brunswick, N.J.: Rutgers Univ. Press, 1958.

Riddel, Joseph N. *The Clairvoyant Eye: The Poetry and Poetics of Wallace Stevens.* Baton Rouge: Louisiana State Univ. Press, 1965.

Stern, Herbert J. *Wallace Stevens: Art of Uncertainty.* Ann Arbor: Univ. of Michigan Press, 1966.

Sukenick, Ronald. *Wallace Stevens: Musing the Obscure.* New York: New York Univ. Press, 1967.

Tindall, William York. *Wallace Stevens.* Univ. of Minnesota Pamphlets on American Writers, No. 11. Minneapolis: Univ. of Minnesota Press, 1961.

Vendler, Helen Hennessy. *On Extended Wings: Wallace Stevens' Longer Poems.* Cambridge, Mass.: Harvard Univ. Press, 1969.

Wallace Stevens: A Collection of Critical Essays. Ed., with an Introduction, by Marie Borroff. Englewood Cliffs, N.J.: Prentice-Hall, 1963.

Walsh, Thomas F. *Concordance to the Poetry of Wallace Stevens.* University Park: Pennsylvania State Univ. Press, 1963.

Wells, Henry W. *Introduction to Wallace Stevens.* Bloomington: Indiana Univ. Press, 1964.

II. OTHER STUDIES

Baird, James. "Transvaluation in the Poetics of Wallace Stevens." *Studies in Honor of John C. Hodges and Alwin Thaler.* Knoxville: Univ. of Tennessee Press, 1961. Pp. 163-173.

Benamou, Michel. "Beyond Emerald or Amethyst: Wallace Stevens and the French Tradition." *Dartmouth College Library Bulletin*, n.s., 4 (December 1961), 60-66.

———. "Le Thème du héros dans la poésie de Wallace Stevens." *Études Anglaises*, 12 (Juillet-Septembre 1959), 222-230.

Benzinger, James. *Images of Eternity: Studies in the Poetry of Religious Vision, from Wordsworth to T. S. Eliot.* Carbondale: Southern Illinois Univ. Press, 1962.

Blackmur, R. P. *Form and Value in Modern Poetry.* Garden City, N.Y.: Doubleday, 1952.

Block, Haskell M. "The Impact of French Symbolism on Modern American Poetry." *The Shaken Realist: Essays in Modern Literature in Honor of Frederick J. Hoffman.* Ed. Melvin J. Friedman and John B. Vickery. Baton Rouge: Louisiana State Univ. Press, 1970. Pp. 165-217.

Bloom, Harold. *The Visionary Company: A Reading of English Romantic Poetry*. Garden City, N.Y.: Doubleday, 1961.

Bryer, Jackson R., and Joseph N. Riddel. "A Checklist of Stevens Criticism." *Twentieth Century Literature*, 8 (October 1962-January 1963), 124-142.

Cambon, Glauco. *The Inclusive Flame: Studies in Modern American Poetry*. Bloomington: Indiana Univ. Press, 1965.

Cunningham, J. V. *Tradition and Poetic Structure*. Denver: Alan Swallow, 1960.

Deutsch, Babette. *Poetry in Our Time: A Critical Survey of Poetry in the English-speaking World, 1900 to 1960*, 2nd ed. Garden City, N. Y.: Doubleday, 1963.

Doggett, Frank. "Abstraction and Wallace Stevens." *Criticism*, 2 (Winter 1960), 23-37.

―――. "This Invented World: Stevens' 'Notes Toward a Supreme Fiction.' " *ELH*, 28 (September 1961), 284-299. Rpt. *The Act of the Mind: Essays on the Poetry of Wallace Stevens*, ed. Pearce and Miller, pp. 13-28.

―――. "Wallace Stevens and the World We Know." *English Journal*, 48 (October 1959), 365-373.

―――. "Wallace Stevens' Later Poetry." *ELH*, 25 (June 1958), 137-154.

―――. "Wallace Stevens' Secrecy of Words: A Note on Import in Poetry." *New England Quarterly*, 31 (September 1958), 375-391.

―――. "Why Read Wallace Stevens?" *Emory Univ. Quarterly*, 18 (Summer 1962), 81-91.

Donoghue, Denis. "Wallace Stevens." *Connoisseurs of Chaos: Ideas of Order in Modern American Poetry*. London: Faber and Faber, 1965.

Donoghue, Denis. "On *Notes Toward a Supreme Fiction.*" *The Ordinary Universe: Soundings in Modern Literature*. London: Faber and Faber, 1968.

Duncan, Joseph E. "Paradise as the Whole Earth." *JHI*, 30 (April-June 1969), 171-186.

Eberhart, Richard. "Emerson and Wallace Stevens." *Literary Review*, 7 (Autumn 1963), 51-71.

Ellmann, Richard. "Wallace Stevens' Ice-Cream." *Kenyon Review*, 19 (Winter 1957), 89-105.

Fuchs, Daniel. "Wallace Stevens and Santayana." *Patterns of Commitment in American Literature*. Ed. Marston Lafrance. Toronto: Univ. of Toronto Press, 1967. Pp. 135-164.

Frye, Northrop. "The Realistic Oriole: A Study of Wallace Stevens." *Hudson Review*, 10 (Autumn 1957), 353-370. Rpt. *Wallace Stevens: A Collection of Critical Essays*, ed. Borroff, pp. 161-176.

Huston, J. Dennis. "*Credences of Summer*: An Analysis." *MP*, 67 (February 1970), 263-272.

Leiter, Louis H. "Sense in Nonsense: Wallace Stevens' 'The Bird with the Coppery, Keen Claws.'" *College English*, 26 (April 1965), 551-554.

MacCaffrey, Isabel G. "The Other Side of Silence: 'Credences of Summer' as an Example." *MLQ*, 30 (September 1969), 417-438.

McFadden, George. "Poet, Nature, and Society in Wallace Stevens." *MLQ*, 23 (September 1962), 263-271.

———. "Probings for an Integration: Color Symbolism in Wallace Stevens." *MP*, 58 (February 1961), 186-193.

McNamara, Peter L. "The Multi-Faceted Blackbird and Wallace Stevens' Poetic Vision." *College English*, 25 (March 1964), 446-448.

Macksey, Richard A. "The Climates of Wallace Stevens." *The Act of the Mind: Essays on the Poetry of Wallace Stevens*, ed. Pearce and Miller, pp. 185-223.

Martz, Louis L. "Wallace Stevens: The World as Meditation." *Yale Review*, n.s., 47 (Summer 1958), 517-536. Rpt. *The Achievement of Wallace Stevens*, ed. Brown and Haller, pp. 211-231; and *Wallace Stevens: A Collection of Critical Essays*, ed. Borroff, pp. 133-150.

————. "The World of Wallace Stevens." *Modern American Poetry: Focus Five*. Ed. B. Rajan. London: Dennis Dobson, 1950. Pp. 94-109.

Miller, J. Hillis. "Wallace Stevens' Poetry of Being." *ELH*, 31 (March 1964), 86-105. Rpt. as "Wallace Stevens." *Poets of Reality: Six Twentieth-Century Writers*. Cambridge, Mass.: The Belknap Press of Harvard Univ. Press, 1965. Pp. 217-284.

Mills, Ralph J., Jr. "Wallace Stevens: The Image of the Rock." *Accent*, 18 (Spring 1958), 75-89. Rpt. *Wallace Stevens: A Collection of Critical Essays*, ed. Borroff, pp. 96-110.

————. "Wallace Stevens and the Poem of Earth." *Gemini/Dialogue*, 3 (January 1960), 20-30.

Mizener, Arthur. "Not in Cold Blood." *Kenyon Review*, 13 (Spring 1951), 218-225.

Moore, Geoffrey. "Wallace Stevens: A Hero of Our Time." *The Great Experiment in American Literature*. Ed. Carl Bode. New York: Frederick A. Praeger, 1961. Pp. 103-132. Rpt. *The Achievement of Wallace Stevens*, ed. Brown and Haller, pp. 249-270.

Morse, Samuel French. " 'Lettres d'un Soldat.' " *Dartmouth College Library Bulletin*, n.s., 4 (December 1961), 44-50.

Morse, Samuel French. "The Motive for Metaphor—Wallace Stevens: His Poetry and His Practice." *Origin* V, 2 (Spring 1952), 3-65.

Pack, Robert. "The Abstracting Imagination of Wallace Stevens: Nothingness and the Hero." *Arizona Quarterly*, 11 (Autumn 1955), 197-209.

————. "Wallace Stevens: The Secular Mystery and the Comic Spirit." *Western Review*, 20 (Autumn 1955), 51-62.

Pearce, Roy Harvey. "Wallace Stevens: The Life of the Imagination." *PMLA*, 66 (September 1951), 561-582. Rpt. *Wallace Stevens: A Collection of Critical Essays*, ed. Borroff, pp. 111-132.

Riddel, Joseph N. "The Contours of Stevens Criticism." *ELH*, 31 (March 1964), 106-138. Rpt. *The Act of the Mind: Essays on the Poetry of Wallace Stevens*, ed. Pearce and Miller, pp. 243-276.

————. "The Metaphysical Changes of Stevens' 'Esthétique du Mal.'" *Twentieth Century Literature*, 7 (July 1961), 64-80.

————. "Wallace Stevens' 'Notes Toward A Supreme Fiction.'" *Wisconsin Studies in Contemporary Literature*, 2 (Spring-Summer 1961), 20-42.

————. "Wallace Stevens' 'Visibility of Thought.'" *PMLA*, 77 (September 1962), 482-498.

Watts, Harold H. "Wallace Stevens and the Rock of Summer." *Kenyon Review*, 14 (Winter 1952), 122-140.

Wentersdorf, Karl P. "Wallace Stevens, Dante Alighieri, and the Emperor." *Twentieth Century Literature*, 13 (January 1968), 197-204.

Young, David P. "A Skeptical Music: Stevens and Santayana." *Criticism*, 7 (Summer 1965), 263-283.

INDEX OF NAMES

INDEX OF POEMS AND ESSAYS
BY WALLACE STEVENS

LIBRARY OF CONGRESS CATALOGING IN PUBLICATION DATA

Morris, Adalaide Kirby, 1942-
   Wallace Stevens: imagination and faith.

   (Princeton essays in literature)
   Bibliography: p.
   1. Stevens, Wallace, 1879-1955.
PS3537.T4753Z679   811'.5'2   73-2495
ISBN 0-691-06265-X